X FACTOR

UNLEASH YOUR
PRESENTING SUPERPOWER

X FACTOR
UNLEASH YOUR PRESENTING SUPERPOWER

YAMINI NAIDU

Published by X factor Publications
Copyright © 2023 Yamini Naidu
Yamini Naidu asserts her right to be known as the author of this work.

ALL RIGHTS RESERVED.

No part of this publication may be reproduced, stored in a retrieval system, or transmitted in any form by any means electronic, mechanical, photocopying, recording or otherwise without the prior consent of the publishers.

Although the author and publisher have made every effort to ensure that the information in this book was correct at press time, the author and publisher do not assume and hereby disclaim any liability to any party for any loss, damage, or disruption caused by errors or omissions, whether such errors or omissions result from negligence, accident or any other cause.

The material in this publication is of the nature of general comment only, and does not represent professional advice. It is not intended to provide specific guidance for particular circumstances and it should not be relied on as the basis for any decision to take action or not take action on any matter, which it covers. Readers should obtain professional advice where appropriate, before making any such decision.

To the maximum extent permitted by law, the author and publisher disclaim all responsibility and liability to any person, arising directly or indirectly from any person taking or not taking action based on the information in this publication.

ISBN: 978-0-6485987-5-6 (paperback)
ISBN: 978-0-6485987-6-3 (eBook)

 A catalogue record for this book is available from the National Library of Australia

Cover, text design and typesetting by Lorna Hendry
Edited by Jem Bates

*In loving memory of Rita Agati,
who had more smarts, sass and
X factor than anyone I know.*

ABOUT THE AUTHOR

Yamini Naidu, CSP*, is the world's only economist turned Bollywood-dancing business storyteller. She pioneered business storytelling in Australia and co-founded Australia's first business storytelling company. She is rated among the top three business storytellers globally. Her clients include Google, Atlassian, Ford Motor Company, Tiffany & Co, Adidas, ANZ and Goldman Sachs. She works at board and CEO level across the world, moving leaders from spreadsheets to stories.

She has authored several books, including *Story Mastery: How leaders supercharge results with storytelling*, published in 2018. *Power Play: Game-changing influence strategies for leaders* and the bestseller *Hooked: How leaders connect, engage and inspire using storytelling* were both published internationally by John Wiley & Sons.

A global citizen, Yamini was born and raised in Mumbai (formerly Bombay) in India. She is a gold medallist from University of Bombay and a scholarship winner and postgraduate from the London School of Economics.

Yamini is a voluntary guide at the National Gallery of Victoria. She has been guiding for over ten years and is proud to be part of the NGV, a Melbourne icon.

Yamini has lived, worked and studied in India, Asia, Europe and the Americas. She now lives in Melbourne, Australia, with her large extended family and a crazy, all-humans-adoring, geriatric cavoodle named Ace.

---

* A CSP designation is the highest honour awarded to speakers across the globe by both Australia's National and Global Professional Speaking bodies. In Australia there are approximately 150 CSPs, only 50 of them female.

WHAT OTHERS SAY

I have been privileged to have a long association with Yamini. She brings a positive spirit and infectious energy to her work and always leaves behind a lasting impression. More than 10 years on, people from my old team still comment on Yamini's engaging educational sessions, with great content and challenging fun exercises that have made a real difference to their ability to connect with people in their lives.
John Burgin, Chairman ICT Committee,
ANZ India Business Chamber

Yamini's ability to help leaders unlock the power of storytelling in a fun and authentic way is inspiring, insightful and transformative. I am forever grateful that our paths crossed many years ago. Yamini has had such an impact on me, and I am sure on many others.
Edweena Stratton, Chief People Officer, Culture Amp

Our Executive Team at Dental Health Services Victoria had the privilege of a Story Telling Masterclass with the amazing Yamini Naidu. The team came away inspired and able to tell their stories in their own voice. We have been putting our new skill to good use to help join the dots for our teams and create authentic connections. The team rated it the best workshop they have done in decades. Thanks, Yamini.
Susan McKee, Chief Executive Officer,
Dental Health Services Victoria

Yamini attended our all-company meeting and showed us not only the importance but also the impact of storytelling. She engaged the whole group from start to finish. She did it in such a wonderful way that had us all thinking hard about how we could tell our own stories; after all, we all have an interesting story to tell!

Allison Rossiter, Managing Director
Roche Diagnostics Australia

I've yet to meet a person who hasn't called themselves 'Yamini's #1 fan' after seeing her speak. She is breathtaking in every way. Authentic and professional, hilarious and insightful, big on inspiration but even bigger on practical value. Audiences don't just learn a few things or feel good for a few hours after seeing Yamini on stage. They find the courage and clarity to make immediate changes in their work, life and relationships, resulting in a tsunami of positive impact in their careers, families, organisations and communities.

If you want a speaker who doesn't just nail the brief, but leaves your audience enthralled, pick up the phone and call her agent ASAP!

Mykel Dixon, award-winning speaker and Creative Leadership Expert, author of *Everyday Creative: A dangerous guide to making magic a work*

Yamini led our leadership team on a storytelling journey which was remarkable in both its insight and impact. Her ability to identify and distil the key elements of a situation, and package these into an engaging narrative, drawing on emotion and instinct as well as logic, is unique in my experience. Yamini transforms the mundane to the inspiring, thereby bringing to life both the story and the storyteller.

Grant Kelley, Chief Executive Officer,
Vicinity Centres Limited

The 'Storytelling for Impact' professional development workshop conducted by Yamini Naidu is essential for anyone aspiring to excellence. 'Telling stories is one of the most powerful means that leaders have to influence, teach, and inspire' (Boris, V. 2017, What Makes Storytelling So Effective for Learning? Harvard Business Publishing, Dec. 20). Yamini effectively demonstrated this through her interactive teaching of the mechanics of visual communication through structuring stories for impact (her compelling 'two bites of the apple' story is just the start), through modelling best practice, and transforming participants through guided activities. She is the powerhouse of the narrative! I rate this as one of the most transformative workshops I have attended.

Dr Margaret Heffernan, OAM, Senior Lecturer,
School of Management RMIT University

Yamini presented an engaging and impactful storytelling masterclass to hundreds of members of our Business Chicks community. She delivered her unique presentation with passion, commitment and beautiful storytelling. The feedback from the audience was overwhelmingly positive — she truly captured people's hearts and minds.

Olivia Ruello, CEO, Business Chicks

We recently used Yamini for our premier client event, where she toured Australia's capital cities presenting to hundreds of our clients. Yamini has a compelling story to tell and one that resonated extremely well with our business clients. Yamini's style is highly engaging and in many ways enchanting, as she shares the secret power of storytelling through practical examples. I would highly recommend Yamini to anyone thinking about how to create greater engagement with their clients or employees.

Don Sillar, Head of Sales, ANZ Private

CONTENTS

Gratitude — 2

PART A
X FACTOR REDEFINED — 7

1. X factor redefined — 8
2. Build your X factor on solid foundations — 33
3. The new model — 47

PART B
DISCOVERING YOUR X FACTOR — 69

4. Quest ahoy — 70
5. Mining for gold — 81
6. Craft your X factor statement — 108

PART C
FUTURE-PROOFING — 139

7. Embrace and showcase — 140
8. Evolve and be future ready — 160
9. The fortune is in prema — 175

Let's connect — 186
Additional resources — 187

GRATITUDE

'Ring of fire' is how I would describe the journey of writing this book.

At midnight on May 1, 2022, I had a near-death experience. I ended up in ER. The doctors, nurses and some of the best health care in the world saved me. Apart from giving birth, I had never been to hospital. I know, I have been amazingly lucky to have enjoyed good health all my life. Knock on wood. Looking back at what happened, the storyteller in me has one tiny regret. My NDE was not accompanied by an out-of-body experience, damn it — that would have made a brilliant story!

I am totally fine now, but at the time the experience was traumatic for both me and my loved ones. For a week I was immobile in bed, unable to use a screen or to read. But I had the trees and street view outside my bedroom window, and my own thoughts. What helped was the love and care of my family. And, most importantly, my work. That I couldn't physically do any work didn't prevent me from busily creating, ideating and writing in my head. Without the fuel for my mind and imagination provided by my work, I would have gone stir crazy. Thinking about and planning this book kept me sane, kept me motivated and kept me going.

The idea for the book was sparked a few years ago. At the Professional Speakers Australia (PSA) Convention in 2020 the amazing Vinh Giang shared a life-changing model. His positioning of the word X factor set my imagination on fire and gave me a new way of looking at my practice. This spark would be on slow burn for two years, fuelling everything I did. Vinh, I am forever indebted to you for your inspiration. *Sashtang Pranam*, Vinh. In India this entails prostrating in thanks before a teacher, honouring their talent and what they have taught us.

Then the wonderful Warwick Merry invited me to present to the Victorian chapter of the PSA. I grappled with how to best serve my fellow speakers. I focused on what I had been obsessing about and designed a presentation on the X factor concept. My audience's overwhelmingly positive response was like champagne for my soul. That 45-minute presentation grew into a keynote, a masterclass and now this book. Watch out, there may be a musical, a documentary and a Netflix series on the way!

While writing this book, what freaked me out was discovering that there is not a single other book on the market for X factor presentations. That means the idea is either brilliant or rubbish. But my clients encouraged me and loved the keynote, the masterclasses and the process. 'It works, hallelujah!' responded one client. The confidence of my clients and my determination to serve my readers kept me strong in the face of the buffeting winds of self-doubt.

But none of this would have been possible without my writer's group, Sandy McDonald, Di Percy, Carolyn Tate and Kath Walters. From conception to the completed book, you were with me every step of the way. The best book birthing partners in the world. Thank you for your generosity in testing the ideas, for allowing your own experiences to be used in the book and for your tough love. All done with humour, kindness and commercial smarts. Seeing your bright faces every Monday morning, sets my week up with sunshine. My one wish for every writer on the planet is that you are lucky enough to find a writing group like mine.

My thanks to Tracey Ezard, Mariam Issa and Sandy McDonald, who let me feature their case studies in my book. Thank you for pure gold. All three of you and your work make the world a better place. And if anyone wants to nourish their soul, do please visit Mariam's open garden in Brighton, Melbourne, Australia.

My safe harbour in all life's storms is my family, my friends and my work. I love my work and recognise and am grateful for the privilege it offers. I often pinch myself that this is work, not my best dream! And my clients make this dream work possible. You book and rebook me and then recommend me to others. I am honoured, humbled and grateful. Your heartfelt word-of-mouth recommendations trump any social media shenanigans. Five stars!

To my friends, especially the GIF Girls (Anna, Kim and Linda), for supporting me wholeheartedly in the rollercoaster ride that is life. Thank you for putting up with my outpourings, random rants and endless GIFs, and for the life advice, love and laughter. Between us it always feels like nothing is too small (bad hair days), too big (life experiences) or too much (BMI and other catastrophes) to share.

To my friend Ila Sachdeva, who showed up in my darkest hour with love, wisdom and homemade *alu parathas* and *rajma chawal*, Indian comfort food and saved me. You are always just a phone call or cup of chai away. Thank you.

But most of all to my family. Your support grounds me and your love gives me wings. Without you, my life would be empty. Because of you my life has love, meaning and endless requests for hot dinners.

Finally, thank you, dear reader, for choosing this book and for taking this first step towards discovering your X factor. I have only one wish for this book — that it serves you well.

PART A
X FACTOR REDEFINED

CHAPTER 1

X FACTOR REDEFINED

What are the first images that flash into your head when you hear the words *X factor*? Maybe it's a glossy TV show, a panel of judges, a gold statue? On the podium stands a clear winner and two other finalists (trying to pretend they're happy for the winner and fake smiling for the camera through their tears). An hour later no one can remember their names. Soon after that, in the sea of other reality TV shows, even the winner's name is washed away, and apart from the occasional Kelly Clarkson or Guy Sebastian we seldom hear from them again.

Or you might think of global superstars like Madonna or RuPaul whose X factor rests on their talent and fame. There's a chicken and egg quality here. You can't tell for sure if their X factor made them famous or fame came first. Either way, their X factor is so great that they are mononyms, known by a single name alone. Traditionally, our X factor lens has been set on zoom. What we see is mega stardom and the debris of reality TV shows.

This zoom setting on our X factor lens distorts our view. The conventional idea that X factor is only for a handful of exceptional people is bullsh%t, done, finished, over. In this book I will blow that myth wide open. There is now a modern X factor, and everyone, *everyone*, has X factor potential. More on that shortly. (Cue suspenseful music.)

But first, let's talk about you. Why did you pick up this book? Perhaps:

- the idea of X factor intrigues you, and you're keen to learn more and to discover *your* X factor
- you want to scoff — *X factor*, you were *born with it!*
- you want to compete on *The X factor* reality show

If you are a presenter, whether novice or master, and you are keen to discover and unleash your X factor, I welcome you with open arms. I also warmly welcome you if you're a scoffer. I love a sceptic. I've thought about you as I wrote and tried to answer your questions. But do challenge the ideas here and play devil's advocate. All I ask is that you keep an open mind and give the book a fair go. The results may surprise you.

This book is for all of you, though not so much if you're hoping for an entrée to the reality TV show *The X factor* or its latest avatar. Stop looking for distractions, go off now and practise your talents, and good luck.

WHY X FACTOR?

For high level business professionals, the ability to present persuasively is an essential part of your job. But do you present, or do you create an audience experience? Hand on your heart, with every presentation do you:

- connect, engage and inspire your audience
- move people to action
- achieve personal and professional impact?

In my experience only the top professional speakers hit these goals consistently with every presentation. If you want to guarantee this outcome, investing your time, money and energy solely in traditional presentation skills is NOT the answer. So what do you need to do better, smarter and differently? You need to unleash your presentation superpower. Excuse me, you may say, superpower? Yes, *superpower*.

I speak professionally for a living and have been doing so for over 15 years. That's like 150 years in ordinary time! I'm an economist by training. Imagine how boring my training made me. All those years ago, when I started my speaking career, I was a very serious speaker, a serious economist (a classic stereotype), and I was living the stereotype (apologies to all my fellow economists). One year I was giving a keynote speech at IBM and as I looked out at the audience I saw a sea of Indian faces, and I thought perhaps my audience would relate to my Indian mum's story. So I took a leap of faith and began: 'I'm an economist by training, and yet I co-founded a company that does business storytelling. I was so excited that I raced home to tell my mum: "Mum, I'm going start a storytelling company." And she replied, "Is that a job? Why can't you be a doctor or something in IT"'. The audience roared with laughter. The room lit up and in that moment my audience and I became one. We connected viscerally.

That day I stumbled onto something important. For me at that time my X factor was *sharing funny stories*. That's what I called it, I didn't use the words X factor. One of my clients even refers to me as 'a funny story speaker'! It never occurred to me that what I was doing lived in a larger context, or was something that could be taught and learned.

Flash forward to March 2020. I was in Adelaide, South Australia, for the PSA Convention. That's an industry event where professional speakers meet and share trade secrets. Vinh Giang, a keynote speaker who commands the international stage, inspiring audiences globally (and is a wonderful human being), said that every presentation should consist of:

- 30% *content*. As experts, you have this.
- 30% *delivery*. Delivery creates the audience experience.
- 30% *inspiration*. Storytelling and humour — yesses. Hooray, happy dance! I have spent my entire career working with leaders on this.

Figure 1.1 The model

What makes up the remaining 10%? This is *X factor*. Vinh's X factor is that he uses magic as his metaphor on stage. He performs magic and card tricks on stage to illustrate some of his messages. It's immersive and captivating to watch.

But why focus on 10%? This 10% is critical for you only if you want to be more than just another presenter —if you want to be a *presentation leader*. A presentation leader achieves personal and professional impact and business results with every presentation. They don't just present, as I said before, they create an audience experience. With every presentation they transform people, organisations and what's possible. Presentation leaders know this 10% is where their competitive edge lies. The 10% X factor unlocks your presentation magic and:

- creates and cements your reputation as a brilliant presenter, inside and outside your organisation
- transforms every presentation so you connect, engage and inspire
- wows peers, clients and boards
- wins that pitch, promotion or business result
- guarantees you are mistaken for a professional speaker (someone who speaks for a living, is paid to speak and speaks full time for their job).

In chaos theory, the butterfly effect refers to the way one small change can kick off a very large variation. A butterfly flapping its wings in Melbourne triggers a tsunami in South America. That is the power of your X factor. Unleashing this butterfly effect can create a new future for your clients, for your organisation and, most of all, for you.

Reliable and referrable

But what about that remaining 90%? In Giang's model, content, delivery and inspiration matter. Content, delivery and inspiration matter. Good content and delivery make up 60% of the job and create *reliable* presenters. Who doesn't like reliable? You value a reliable watch and phone and service provider. In the presentation game, reliable earns permission to sit at the table. It's the baseline.

Inspiration (storytelling and humour), the next 30% in the model, creates *referrable* presenters. Inspiring presenters build a great reputation inside and outside organisations. As an inspiring presenter, you generate excellent word of mouth. People want to hear you present. They always mention your name in the line-up for business-critical pitches, and clients want to do business with you.

You can become the face of your organisation. With good content and delivery, clients will *like* you. Add inspiration and clients *love* you.

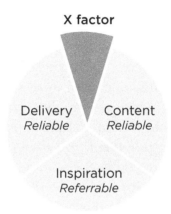

Figure 1.2 X factor model

Raving fans

X factor creates raving fans. Your clients don't just like you or love you, they can't live without you. You are their first port of call. Clients don't even consider your competitors. Whenever your area of expertise comes up, yours is the first, often the only, name on their lips. Clients might say something like, 'Yes, there are many people in that field, but if you want to work with the best, then there's only [*insert your name here*]'. Take a moment to savour that feeling.

Content plus delivery plus inspiration makes you an inspiring presenter. You absolutely need this holy trinity.

But to be a presentation leader, you can't stop there. It's like planting your flag at Mount Everest base camp because you didn't know the summit was still 20.5 kilometres away.

It's also deeply uncool to plant your flag at base camp. And unless you are a comedian, a classic couch potato or making an ironic TikTok video, no one is interested in your struggles to reach base camp. X factor is the difference between reaching base camp and planting your flag on the summit.

In addition to the holy trinity of content, delivery and inspiration, you need X factor, because X factor makes you an unforgettable presenter. In an age when anyone can find anything they need to know with a Google search, just providing information, even in an inspiring way, is no longer enough. Audiences don't just want infotainment. They want presenters to enthral them. To be enthralled is to be temporarily spellbound. When you enthral them, the audience forgets everything else; they are completely in the moment, connected, listening and absorbing your messages. And your X factor can do this heavy lifting for you. If you know how to use it.

Carla Harris is the Vice Chairman of Wealth Management and Senior Client Advisor at Morgan Stanley. She is a Wall Street heavy hitter. I came across the terms *performance currency* and *relationship currency* in her book *Strategize to Win: The New Way to Start Out, Step Up or Start Over in Your Career*.

Harris explains how you build performance currency when you get your job done, when you deliver results; but when you connect with people, when you invest in relationships, you build relationship currency. As a professional you need both. Early in your career, your performance currency has a higher value. As you take on more senior and leadership roles, your relationship currency has a higher value. Your X factor is a superhero that helps you build your relationship currency. People want to connect with you, seek your advice and recommend you. Clients rave about you. Relationships become easy, effortless and rewarding.

Why else is this 10% X factor non-negotiable?

Reference points

Imagine winning an Olympic medal. How would you feel? Ecstatic, over the moon, the happiest person on Earth? Sadly, this doesn't always seem to be the case. The gold medallist's smile can be seen from the moon (they have deservedly made a place in history). What's surprising is that bronze medallists smile just as widely. They are as happy as the gold winners, if not happier. The silver medallist looks the least happy and feels worse off than the bronze medallist. Behavioural economics uses *reference points theory* to explain why.

Reference points help you assess your accomplishments. Of course, silver medallists have their eye on gold. Their reference point is higher, on what could have been. Bronze medallists feel, phew, they won a medal, beating so many other competitors. Their reference point is lower. They are spared the fate they narrowly missed, not getting a medal at all. Consider swimmer Fu Yuanhui's reaction at the Rio Olympics. Shock, surprise, delight when she found out from a reporter that she had won a bronze medal in the women's 100-metre backstroke, when she thought she had missed out. This delightful moment went viral. Fu Yuanhui won the world's heart and she has become one of China's most popular sportspeople. All without winning a gold medal.

But sadly, for silver medallists the pain doesn't stop when they step off the podium, and sometimes it never ebbs away. They often feel gutted over this loss for the rest of their lives. In the 1912 Olympics, Abel Kiviat, an American middle-distance runner, lost the 1500-metre race by one-tenth of a second. In an interview with *The Los Angeles Times* many years later, when he was a 91-year-old, he said, 'I wake up sometimes and say, "What the heck happened to me?" It's like a nightmare.'

You don't ever want to wind up in the land of *if only* and *why didn't I*. You never want to lose to a competitor by a tenth of a second, when that's all that separates second best from best. Your X factor holds the magic key. In presenting, X factor separates entertaining from enthralling, silver medallists from gold medallists, your competitors from you.

But why do so many presenters feel this 10% is out of reach? Possibly they don't know about X factor's role in presentations. Maybe they have believed the myths about X factor, or maybe they have never thought about their X factor before.

REDEFINING X FACTOR

The monstrous barrier that limits most professionals is their traditional, narrow view of X factor and the notion that it is accessible by only a handful of people. Time to redefine X factor.

Shaking our tail feathers

The X factor concept has been hijacked by reality TV shows with their slick, exuberant showmanship, their super-sized, glamorous 'stars', wannabe aspirants, sequins flashing, shaking their tail feathers. This is something, you imagine, they are born with. X factor is presence. When someone with this quality enters a room, you expect the earth to tremble; when they smile the light glints off their teeth, dazzling you.

This conventional, old-fashioned view of X factor is dated. It is time for us to take it back and redefine it, as this view is distancing for an audience and has little relevance in our professional context. When you zoom out from this myopic view, what you see is a whole new world of possibilities.

For professional presenters, X factor can be one uncommon or special thing. It can be a talent for remembering the names of people when all the rest of us forget. Or being empathetic to the point of almost channelling other people's feelings. Or being able to do complex calculations in your head effortlessly. For Danielle Dobson, a lifestyle photographer based in Melbourne, Australia, photos are 'the closest thing to real-life magic'. Dobson connects to her craft as an expression of something magical — that's her X factor right there. I have never heard any other photographer describe themselves like this. It is distinctive and memorable and born out of the way she works.

For professional speakers, X factor is their advantage, a skill they have honed. It could be the quality of their ideas, or it could be their stage presence or theatrical delivery that rivets their audience through funny storytelling. Dr Shefali Tsabary, a *New York Times* bestselling author and international speaker, is 'a clinical psychologist and a wisdom teacher specialising in integrating Western psychology and Eastern philosophy'. Her marriage of science and ancient wisdom, east and west, is pure X factor for a professional speaker.

Then there are show-biz performers. X factor isn't just 10% of their job, it's their *entire* job. Comedy superstar Trevor Noah hosts *The Daily Show*. In the sea of American late-night TV shows, Noah stands out. He is biracial (born to a white father and a black mother), a migrant from South Africa, and young. His blend of storytelling, satire and comedy is alluring and refreshing, winning him global cult status.

In geometry, a line extends infinitely in both directions. The X factor spectrum is also infinite, and you can find your own place, whether as a presenter, a professional speaker or a show-biz performer. The X factor spectrum isn't just limited to celebrity performers like Noah. I have shared examples above where professionals and speakers also have X factor.

What unites all presenters, professional speakers and show-biz performers is they all bring something special to the table and are committed to *serve* their audience. Your X factor is something you do *for* rather than *to* an audience. And there, you never thought you would feature on the same continuum as Ricky Gervais. Group hug. This is a moment!

As a presenter, you have the opportunity to discover a new X factor. A different kind of X factor that has been pretty much invisible to you until now. Here's a contrast table that compares the old and the new.

Traditional X factor	Modern X factor
All about me	Serves my audience, message and purpose
Show-stopping sauce	Special sauce
Sequins, tail feathers, glitter	Optional, and only if it serves my audience and message
Big, bold; can intimidate	Can be quiet, small, intimate; creates connection
Innate — you have it or you don't	Complex but definable and teachable
Exclusive — only for a handful	Everyone has X factor potential

Figure 1.3 Traditional versus modern X factor

Without overstating this point, discovering X factor today is comparable to how Sir Isaac Newton must have felt when he 'discovered' the universal theory of gravity, which revolutionised how humanity viewed the world.

This new view of X factor can revolutionise your world and what is possible for you. You are no longer chasing after it or terrified by its absence, seeing it as this elusive, impossibly distant goal. It's not about winning a talent show or becoming the Beyoncé of business, and it's not the reward of a tiny, exclusive elite. Rather, it's something that is immediately achievable and applicable in your context. You haven't done it yet, but it is doable. It is your edge.

And the magic doesn't stop with your presentations and professional life. It can spill over into your personal life. It can help you dazzle your date and wow friends at dinner parties.

But wait, there's more. X factor is also your safety net. It's like a loyal, trusted friend who never lets you down. It is your hammock on a bad day when you feel like you can barely stand, let alone present to an audience. Even on your darkest day you can say to yourself, ah, but I do have my X factor. I always ask insightful questions or I connect empathetically with clients, or I create high-value models. So what stops us from stepping into this bold new future?

Risky business

According to the Himalayan Database, as of January 2019, just 5,294 mountaineers have successfully summitted Everest. I was gobsmacked by that number, expecting it to be much higher. It makes sense, though, as the risks are significant, but then so is the reward.

Finding, owning and being known for your X factor is hard. Let's not shy away from this. **But finding and unleashing your X factor will forever change how you present, the impact you have and the shift you can create in your world.**

Finding and unleashing your X factor in business can be risky, but only if done badly by drawing on the old stereotypes. What is far riskier is going through the rest of your personal and professional life without discovering and implementing your X factor, thereby condemning yourself and your audience to more of the same. Presentations with messages that sink without a trace; opportunities for impact, sales and revenue — lost; your professional reputation unfulfilled. Lack of X factor will reduce a presenter's opportunities for promotion and for shifting client relationships from transactional to transformational.

To quote Super Mario, same is lame. Same sets us up for a losing streak into the future. The greatest risk with regard to X factor is if it's never discovered. On the plus side, **X factor can attract blue-chip clients, deliver massive impact, boost sales, lift revenue, and create a lasting personal and professional legacy.** And exploring and experimenting with your X factor is fun and an adventure, I promise.

In his 2022 bestseller *The Power of Regret*, Daniel Pink argues, '... we are much more likely to regret the chances we *didn't take* than the chances we did take ... It doesn't matter what the forgone opportunity is, whether it's our education, our work, or our love life, the regret lingers in the same way'. Don't let that be your regret with your X factor.

A wish list

You may worry that finding your X factor will take years and years of hard work and talent. What if this book is part of a trilogy, a year-long festival or eight seasons on Netflix?

As my reader, I know you are sophisticated and smart (yes, blatant flattery). So you already know that unearthing an X factor that serves your audience and message and keeps people on the edge of their seats will require hard work. But help is at hand.

I have made some assumptions about you. I know you are, like my clients, time poor and juggling complex priorities, and you want results. You know X factor is important but you cannot dedicate endless time to skilling. Perhaps you are sceptical because you have invested in many presentation skills courses in the past and you know any change is slow. If you are like the professionals I work with, you also want to be authentic. You're not looking for an extreme makeover. You have a hunger to stand out but are unsure of how to channel that in your next presentation. Most of all, you want to be memorable.

This sounds like a giant wish list, but it can be done. In this book I have compressed my 15 years of X factor building expertise, my 10,000-plus hours of work and decades of deep practice at the coal face with clients just like you. This book provides the answers, the steps and the shortcuts, so you can experience X factor success fast while staying true to who you are. It sets you up for great results and shows you how you can do this safely and smartly. More on this in later chapters.

Now let's dissect *X factor*.

ANATOMY OF X FACTOR

Your X factor is born from your own unique set of skills, talents, lived experiences, quirks, hobbies and interests. In later chapters I will show you how you can discover this special combination for yourself. My work has uncovered that X factor has both a surface structure and a deep structure. Our audience experiences only the surface structure, what happens on stage. It is like the magic a magician creates.

Meet me at the intersection

As a presenter, you unearth your X factor by understanding what's beneath the surface, the deep structure that creates the magic, the behind-the-scenes process, which has four key sources that anyone can tap into.

1. What gives modern X factor its depth is your intent —your *purpose*. It could be to make your message memorable, resonate with your audience and help people understand your content. I teach some of my content through Bollywood dancing. My clients tell me this helps people remember key messages, because they associate them with the dance moves and have fun at the same time as learning
2. Modern X factor must help your audience understand your message. This is often referred to as being *in service* of your audience. Ask yourself, 'Does my X factor serve the room?' You might love belting out a tune, or wearing a kooky costume, or rattling off rhyming couplets, but will any of these serve your audience? That is the litmus test for any X factor. Service keeps you grounded and sets you up for success in any professional context. It

also stops you veering down endless rabbit holes and helps you make the right decisions around choosing your X factor.
3. Does your X factor make your presentation better, richer, deeper? In other words, does it *add value* to your presentation for your clients and for your business? If you removed your X factor content from your presentation, would this reduce the value or impact of the presentation? Would its inclusion improve attention, retention and results?
4. Most importantly, X factor challenges you to find and share *something that you love*. It must pass the heart test. Rumi, the thirteenth-century Persian poet, mystic and Sufi, tells us, 'Go into the heart to touch the sky'. There you'll find something that lights you up. As I have said, it doesn't have to be big. It can be something as small as colour. Naomi Simson is an Australian businessperson, entrepreneur and the founder of RedBalloon. Simson only wears red; it is her signature look. She says the colour is her public uniform and helps identify what she stands for.

Pulling these ideas together, figure 1.4 illustrates this modern X factor. It is multidimensional and lives at the intersection of purpose, service, value and uniqueness, which gives it distinctiveness, depth and richness.

Think of these concepts, not as straitjackets, but as guides.

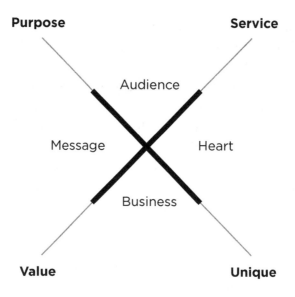

Figure 1.4 X factor — the intersection

Creating the magic

While these guides are universal, they are also personal. What creates the magic in your X factor is that you discover what makes you different from everyone else in a warm and relatable way. Figure 1.5 suggests what you might find when you zoom in to unique — your deepest self.

Your deepest self is rich and distinctive. This means:

1. You must enjoy your X factor. Fun is compulsory. A sparkle in your eyes, a bounce in your step and a smile on your lips all add magic to your X factor. You can't be intense, hair standing up, a stress bunny with a grim countenance. **Being too serious is kryptonite for your X factor.**

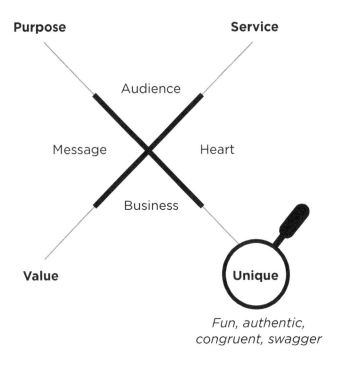

Figure 1.5 Zooming into your deepest self

2. Your X factor must be *authentic*. The difference in value between a painting with the authentication 'From the hand of Rembrandt' and one painted 'in the manner of Rembrandt' is vast. Your X factor can't be derivative, contrived or manufactured. You live in a world with a fierce cancel culture; your audiences are sophisticated and very sensitive about appropriation. I'll show you how to discover and protect your authenticity and know that no one can imitate you.
3. Your X factor must be *congruent* with who you are, demonstrating your integrity. It lets you be the best version of yourself when presenting, but it is something you can sustain on and off stage. It works even if you are

an introvert, naturally quiet or soft-spoken. The light of your X factor never fades, even when the curtain comes down.
4. What puts the X into X factor is some *swagger*. You must own it. No point in trying too hard or being hesitant. Swagger comes from doing the work, road testing what you have and trusting yourself. It is likeable confidence, not arrogance. Ash Barty is a three-time Grand Slam tennis singles champion and 2022 Wimbledon and Australian Open champion. Barty said she won because she was enjoying it. This is a champion X factor move.

When exploring these depths to uncover your X factor, it is like looking closely at thousands of dots of a pointillist image. You can't see the full picture yet. That will take shape in later chapters as you step back and view your X factor with a masterful eye.

Now it's time now to put on your big-person pants.

My inner what?

I'm going to say something that may make you uncomfortable, but it needs to be said (honesty being the best policy). **X factor requires you to lean into your inner artist.** I don't know what this word conjures up for you but I want to assure you this doesn't mean turning into someone you're not. What it means is tapping into something singular, individual and creative that you must bring to your presentations.

Your X factor is an expression of you. In our professional world, where so much is vanilla, now more than ever the world is hungry for the spice of your X factor. Your audience is desperate and you are remarkable; it's a perfect match. There's only one of you in the world. And you have this book to guide you. You are in exactly the right place at the right time.

To define something, bobbing above the water like a disturbed buoy, is also to identify what it is not. X factor is not about seeking audience approval. When an audience applauds you, when they laugh at your jokes, it feels good. That's natural, you're human. If used well, your X factor will help make both you and your presentations more likeable and memorable. But popularity and audience approval are not the results you are aiming for. They are simply happy by-products of what you do well, which is to serve your audience with your X factor.

Does your X factor help your audience understand, connect with and remember your message? That's the acid test. Everything you do must be in service. Period. On this my research and experience through reading, presenting, interviewing and working with clients at the coal face is conclusive.

Everyone has X factor potential. But don't just take my word for it. Let's do a simple test to establish where you are with your X factor. You could be:

- **Fuzzy.** You aren't sure. Your X factor, like a shy tortoise, has yet to emerge from its shell. That's totally fine. This book was written for you.
- **Finding.** You are bursting with and exploring possibilities. You're mining for gold. Hooray, this book will help you get there faster.
- **Frolicking.** You are among that lucky few: you totally know, own and are known for your X factor. A warm welcome to you too, because you are smart enough to know that even if you are frolicking in X factor, there's always more to learn. X factor evolves, as I will shortly explain.

Take a moment now to mark where you are with your X factor. Do this again when you reach the end of the book. It is the best measure of your progress and success. Once you are clear on your current location, you are ready to set out on your quest to find your X factor.

TREASURE MAP

You'll go hunting for your X factor through your personal and professional experiences and much more. There's no corner you won't poke your nose into, no potential X factor opportunity you don't double down on, no star you don't reach out for in your quest. And this book is your treasure map. Follow it and X factor treasures are guaranteed.

Here I want to make a confession, because I believe it's always good to begin a relationship with a clean slate. I have made the following assumptions about you, dear reader:

- You are keen to learn.
- You don't want me to just talk about X factor; you want practical, how-to steps to follow.
- You'd like examples from professionals like you.
- You also want to learn X factor cautions to help you avoid any traps.
- You insist that the learning be fun.
- You are big enough for tough love.
- You are smart enough to take this, do the work and apply it in your own context.

Ticked these boxes? Hooray! Keep in mind that this book is developed in a linear way. The learning and insights it offers build cumulatively, like maths, expanding on what came before, so reading the chapters in order is the key. You don't want to be like the kid who skipped school the day they covered fractions and struggles with fractions for the rest of their life. Once you've finished it, you can dip back in and out as you please, revisiting sections when they are most relevant to your own journey.

Sometimes I suggest micro actions to take immediately to help unlock your X factor. Please read these thoughtfully and consider how you might act on them. In some chapters, I recommend specific exercises. These may not always be fun but are not optional. Follow the process I have developed and tested. It works and finding your X factor depends on it.

Below I invite you to accept the multiple ways in which X factor is used in this book. This isn't to be difficult or quirky, but to recognise the multifaceted nature of X factor.

RED FLAG: CONTRARY IDEAS AHEAD

How many shapes are there? This sounds like a simple maths question, but it's something that has puzzled mathematicians forever. The answer is an infinite number.

X factor too can encompass infinite meanings, possibilities, variations. It's a shapeshifter. It can morph endlessly, changing form or identity. Our redefinition is dense and layered to accommodate this. I can't ignore this reality, even though a narrow definition would make life so much simpler.

X factor conventionally can relate to a single word, a phrase, a statement or one of several statements; it can flag the application of a skill or talent, or draw on a story, a song, a hobby. You'll find it expressed as a singular, concrete idea or as a mix of many things (a multiplicity). The possibilities are limitless. This sounds head-bangingly frustrating and throw-book-against-wall exasperating. But don't despair, and please don't hurl either head or book at said wall, as there is a solution to this predicament.

> ## Developing your X factor
>
> In this book you develop your X factor as a presentation superpower, and I'll help you build your own, singular X factor.
>
> I'll guide you towards crafting your X factor as a statement that embodies three ideas that best represent you, combined to create a portrait or representation that best expresses you — in my case, for example, 'the world's only economist turned Bollywood-dancing business storyteller'.
>
> The simplest way to wrap your head around this is to think of your X factor statement as a personal tag line.

This distilling of your X factor matters. Why? Because it matters to the people you serve. It gives you one way (not the only way) of expressing something that is notoriously hard to pin down.

The process I have developed, researched and tested in this book will deliver on that. I don't claim it is the only or even the best way to get there, but it is simple to follow and effective, and my clients consistently tell me it delivers great results every time. **When your X factor statement combines three things, it becomes a powerhouse that transforms your presentations, your professional life and your identity.** Through this book you will find out how.

Once you have nailed this statement, it can change not just your presentations but your world and your understanding of what's possible. You'll also understand that the work is never done. The difference between the old view of X factor and the modern X factor is that this X factor is tangible, it is learnable and it evolves. So yes, your X factor is not static and not simply one thing; it changes over time just as you change. It gets more nuanced, richer and more intimate as you become more confident at being you on stage. X factor is something intimate about you that you're willing to share. (Don't let that spook you. I'll show you how to do this safely and elegantly.) For me it's my love of Bollywood dancing.

Your personal tag line is not the only interpretation of X factor, but it is a practical interpretation that allows you to start the journey and keep evolving. I encourage you to keep deepening your X factor statement over time. Never shut the door on new possibilities around how you can express X factor. Figure 1.6 illustrates my journey. Starting with business storyteller, I moved deeper into my authentic self with Bollywood dancing. Later I will share how this evolved and I arrived at Bollywood dancing.

Figure 1.6 Snapshot view of my X factor journey

Iconic American author, F. Scott Fitzgerald, famously wrote, 'The test of a first-rate intelligence is the ability to hold two opposing ideas in mind at the same time and still retain the ability to function'.

When you encounter the diverse ways I use the words X factor in this book, instead of feeling frustrated, I suggest you simply nod your head sagely, think, 'ah, X factor, you shapeshifter,' and pat yourself on the back for your keen intelligence.

HELP IS AT HAND

Understand, dear reader, that you are never alone on this journey. Links to a vault of online resources are included throughout the book, and you can download what you need to.

I make the work easy and even exciting, but for this book (like any other such book, tool or system) to produce results, you must do the work. This is the only commitment you need to make.

Know that I am also only an email or LinkedIn request away. So please reach out and let me know how I can help. This is my world and I love it. I offer keynotes, masterclasses and workshops on X factor. I work with leaders, leadership teams and brands helping them find their X factor. I am creating a movement of presenters with X factor!

We are at the crossroads now. If you are ready to do the work with me, I promise you a magic carpet ride into an exciting future. You will laugh, learn and taste success every inch of the way. I'll hold your hand and make this journey not just possible but easy.

So are you ready to unleash your X factor, your presentation superpower? Group hug. Swipe right. Welcome to a new world.

You can also access rich resources on specific topics you want to know more about by scannng this QR code or going to **xfactor.yamininaidu.com.au**.

CHAPTER 2

BUILD YOUR X FACTOR ON SOLID FOUNDATIONS

Imagine you're travelling to Paris. (I did say there's nowhere you won't go to find your X factor.) What's one of the first images that pops into your head? Is it the Eiffel Tower? When first built this iconic landmark stood at 312 metres tall, but recently it grew by another 20 feet or so courtesy of a new communications antenna. Who knows how much higher it may reach in the future thanks to advancing technology and the robustness of its deep foundations.

As a presenter you may be doing all the right things, yet there is always room to grow, to learn and try something different. Before I turn to growth, though, let me call out some elephants in the room, some things that in my experience are not working in more traditional ways of presenting.

THE RUMBLING OF THE HERD

A few years ago I went to my daughter's school for an information evening. Midway through the evening a parenting expert took the stage, and every parent in the room rolled their eyes. Sensing their displeasure, the expert began, 'You're probably thinking, not another parenting expert, will I ever get home?' The guilty audience burst out laughing.

She then took it a step further, admitting, 'As a parent myself, I've often felt this too. We all know that parenting is the toughest job on earth. It's been said, "You can learn many things from children". How much patience do you have, for instance? So I'm here to share some tips with you that we, as parents, can all use on days when our patience is in short supply. As parents of teenagers, you will have lots of these days'. She invited the elephants into the room and addressed them to heartfelt applause.

Novelist Ellen Wittlinger said, 'When there's an elephant in the room you can't pretend it's not there and just discuss the ants'. What are some of the elephants in the room in terms of what happens either to you or to people you know when they present? (In other words, why do so many presentations suck?)

Sparkly to shrink-wrapped

Many years ago I was at a pharmacy conference. At dinner a witty, charming pharmacy rep entertained us throughout the evening with sparkly anecdotes and well-timed gags that were empathetic and inclusive. All the other tables were looking towards our table enviously, wishing they were seated with him. Such a memorable dinner.

The next morning, the rep stood up to make his presentation to a packed conference room. There was a buzz of excitement and people were leaning in with anticipation, a smile already playing on their lips. We were so sure his presentation would be the highlight of the conference that no one wanted to miss a word. Then he started and our excitement quickly turned to surprise and dismay, even shock. Was this stiff, formal, over-serious stranger the same person whose wit had dazzled everyone the previous evening?

Why does this happen again and again? Presenting is a time in your professional life when you are at your most vulnerable. You must perform or 'die'. Our two biggest fears as adults are of failing and of embarrassing ourselves IN PUBLIC! And every presentation offers both these opportunities on a silver platter. To add to this potent mix, the moment you stand up to speak all your other insecurities come bubbling to the surface. Will they like me? Did I prepare enough? Hope my slides work. I should have worn the other outfit.

Most of us respond to this pressure by seeking safety in morphing into a shrink-wrapped, low-resolution version of ourselves. Which is why you often see funny, animated people become wooden and robotic when presenting. Then you discover that training can help you.

The merry-go-round

Skilling and training are important. How many presentation skills training programs, workshops, masterclasses or seminars have you already participated in? For most professionals the answer is usually somewhere between some and too many. Although you learn something each time, it seems like a big investment for low returns.

While this training is excellent, valuable and much needed, presentation courses too often have a cookie-cutter approach. Stand here, look there, lower your voice. If that's not who you are, when the spotlight shines on you, you return to safety and a 'shrink-wrapped' version of you.

You may also feel you never seem to get off this training bandwagon. While the strategies and techniques may be good and effective, they depend on you implementing them.

The other challenge is remembering and applying what you learn. Everything seems like a good idea in the workshops, but once outside, real life hits you and it all becomes too hard. Or you make small, incremental changes, but the opportunity to win that pitch or promotion arrives before you are match fit. You're playing a long game. What's scary is that at this snail's pace of improvement you may not realise your full potential before it's time to retire!

The dentist's chair

What do you do when you're bumped off two flights and stuck in a deserted Las Vegas airport overnight? Shoot a music video on your iPhone, lip-syncing Celine Dion's 'All by Myself' to share with your friends, of course. This is what Dion super-fan Richard Dunn did, and it amazed him when his video went viral, turning him into an overnight internet sensation. While this is a novel way to channel boredom, what made it work?

Richard Dunn's advice? Start by being true to yourself. What do you enjoy doing? Genuine passion for what you're doing always shines through. Dunn made his video to give his friends a laugh. Simple, clear intent. He is no longer all by himself. Celine Dion made a response video, saying how much she loved Richard's video and invited him to her show in Las Vegas. Happy ending!

In a world where so much is spin, manufactured and contrived, authenticity stands out like a beacon. Leaders and professionals tell me they want to be authentic to their inner self, not to transform themselves dramatically. Yet the worst advice to give a presenter is to 'be yourself'. This is like asking a patient to relax in a dentist's chair.

People are interested in the real you. Writer and professor of literature Joseph Campbell said, 'The privilege of a lifetime is being who you are'. People are interested in who you are and why this presentation is important to you.

So how to convey this well? Here's a distinction that will help. We have spent eons asking the wrong question. **It isn't how to be yourself, but how to be *the best version of yourself*, even under performance pressure.** Figure 2.1 shows how presenters respond differently to the pressure of presenting.

Figure 2.1 Presentation performance pressure response

At bottom left are presenters who respond by turning into a shrink-wrapped version of themselves. At bottom right are presenters who stumble through, stressed because the stakes are high. Feeling a certain amount of nervousness is normal for most presenters, but stressing out during a presentation can see you speaking super-fast, breathlessly racing through your slides. No one likes to watch a stressed presenter; as audience members, we are all empaths and feed off this anxious energy, ending up feeling anxious ourselves.

At top left are seasoned presenters who have done lots of presentation skills training and have practised their presentation. They are word perfect but depend heavily on their script and slides. They are smooth, but sometimes this can leave an audience feeling detached or like they have seen it all before.

When you learn to be the shiniest, sparkliest version of yourself even under performance pressure, your presentation comes across as effortless, natural. You connect with your audience as you would in a conversation. Under performance pressure, you learn not to revert to the baseline but instead to aim for the best version of yourself, to amplify your best self (at the top right— sensational!).

Don't waste time just being you (sorry, I know you're a lovely person). Rather, work on being the best version of you, this sparkly, high-res, sensational version of you.

IMAGINE YOU UNLIMITED

Imagine this new world. Where with every presentation you are sensational. Professional results, standing ovations, raving fans. It will help you bust through to the 90% high bar and reach the top.

So what makes a top presenter?

Be memorable

In their bestseller *Made to Stick*, Chip and Dan Heath ask us to perform this test with our communication. *Do people understand what I'm saying? Will they remember it after and be able to retell it?* That's the power of being memorable.

Yet this is impossible when you do what everyone else is doing, taking what is considered a professional approach, rinse and repeat. Hand on your heart, how many presentations do you remember the day after the event, in a week's time or a year later? The answer is probably somewhere between zero and one.

Being memorable involves risk taking. Predictability is a death sentence for every presentation. It's the boredom that can kill off your audience's attention. Conventional presentation skills training can see you merge in with other presenters, instead of standing out and being memorable.

Leave a legacy

In his 2006 TED Talk, Sir Ken Robinson made an entertaining and profoundly moving case for creating an education system that nurtures rather than undermines creativity. His work has prompted the global education community to re-evaluate how we nurture and grow creativity in children. His talk and work have forced us all —especially governments, teaching institutions and educators — to rethink the role of education in our society. What Robinson did was create a legacy.

Welcome to the shifted role of the presenter, from merely providing information to creating relevance and meaning. As a presenter you'd love your key presentation to live on after you have left the room, the organisation and, dare I say it, the planet.

When I worked in a corporate organisation, my boss once said, 'When people leave, it's like taking your hand out of a bucket of water — that's the difference you've made to the bucket of water.' She was suggesting that a measure of how little they'd be missed was that no evidence of them would remain. So cynical, but so often true. Even if you are a 100% committed to your work, always do your best and are a star performer, even if you have a super-sized ego, this is a moment of humble reckoning. Imagine instead that every presentation builds your reputation and helps create a legacy that lasts long into the future.

Business results

We have probably never met, but I know that your company's business future is right there in your hands. It is professionals like you who build a future that otherwise wouldn't come about, and every presentation you give is an opportunity to contribute to this future, create impact and deliver business results.

Every presentation is an opportunity, whether seized or missed, to generate business results, whatever this looks like for you in your context. It could be nailing that team meeting, having your idea selected or winning that multimillion-dollar client contract. Or – most important – winning people's hearts and minds with every presentation.

A few years ago I featured in an *AFR Boss Magazine* story, along with three of my corporate clients, Accenture, NAB and Ericsson. The article detailed my work in business storytelling. The then Managing Director of Accenture, Jack Percy, is quoted as saying 'Storytelling doubled our revenue'. You read that right. At Accenture during Percy's tenure, it was like storytelling became the organisation's X factor. In hallway conversations, in team and client meetings, in proposals and pitches, the leaders started using stories. That's the power of X factor unleashed. It produces business results on steroids.

So, I invite you to a new world of possibility. A world where, with every presentation, you are memorable, building a legacy and delivering business results. Most of all, this new world allows you to channel who you are in a way that is authentic, fresh and exciting for both you and your audience. Imagine You Unlimited.

To give you a sense of what is possible, let me introduce you to a fellow speaker, Judson Laipply. It's the early 2000s and Laipply is mulling over a word of advice from his speaking mentor: 'Judson, you need something unique, your *thing*.' But he didn't have a thing, nor did he have any idea what his thing could be.

One day at a gig he watched a comedian demonstrating how people dance badly at weddings, and he had a brainwave. He put together key dance moves with music and rehearsed. A few weeks later at the end of his keynote titled 'Life Is Change', for the first time Judson pulled off 12 dance moves through the ages, showing the evolution of dance. He used dance as a metaphor, forever overturning how the audience saw change. Judson discovered his X factor and made internet history.

Judson's dance video became YouTube's first viral video, and he became YouTube's first star. A big round of applause for Judson. He had broken into the corporate market, his revenue exploded and he was flown all over America on private jets. Yet he had started his journey with a small first (dance) step.

This is the first step in your journey to discovering your X factor and You Unlimited.

WHAT HOLDS YOU BACK?

In school in India my maths teacher once pointed to a row of children and asked a question. Every child in the row promptly, as if on comedic cue, turned to the child behind them, as if to suggest the question was for them. Then the next row did the same, until the child sitting in the last row turned to the wall, happy to defer to an inanimate object! We play the same game as adults when we avoid stepping up and owning our X factor.

The whole hog and quarter hog

My clients tell me that they frequently worry that any real change will involve an extreme makeover. But what if you shifted your mode of thinking and saw your X factor quest as a series of small, doable steps, rather than a sudden, life-changing transformation that could cause even the hardiest to baulk.

In their wonderful award-winning book *This Working Life*, Lisa Leong and Monique Ross offer this advice for people seeking career transition. Don't think you have to go the whole hog. You can go the half hog, or even the quarter hog. I love this idea, because it offers a practical solution to many of the problems of making significant change. It gives you permission to start small and apply that wonderful philosophy of test, try and see.

How can you begin quarter hogging? Being a research nerd, that's where I went looking for answers. Katy Milkman is the James G. Dinan Professor at the Wharton School of the University of Pennsylvania. Milkman recommends that instead of selecting the most punishing regime and going hell for leather, you make it fun! In her book *How to Change:*

The Science of Getting from Where You Are to Where You Want to Be, she describes the concept of 'temptation bundling'.

Temptation bundling means linking habit building to something you enjoy — watching your favourite Netflix show only after exercising, for example. Milkman says two key challenges of behavioural change are boredom and lack of instant gratification. Introducing instant interim rewards overcomes these challenges, which is why you will be doing this on our X factor quest.

But we can all slip up as we make changes. Researchers Marissa A. Sharif and Suzanne B. Shu have a nifty solution. They recommend 'emergency reserves'. Give yourself a couple of get-out-of-jail-free cards, so when you slip up, you can draw on emergency reserves to help you forgive yourself and get back on track.

Here's how your get-out-of-jail-free cards also help you counter what marketers call 'the what the hell effect'. You eat something unhealthy, then write off your whole day or diet with a 'what the hell'. Or you start to read a business book determined to learn something new but discard it after 40 pages thinking 'what the hell' and go back to checking your social media. Recognising the start of this 'what the hell' spiral, using one of your get-out-of-jail-free cards and being able to reset will help you on your journey.

Most importantly, discovering your X factor is not always about hustle and hard work; it's also about heart, so be kind to yourself. Self-compassion research is an emerging field. It turns out that being kind to yourself is the best thing you can do to support any behavioural change as well as your long-term physical and mental health. And it's totally free. You will enjoy lots of love, kindness and group hugs throughout this journey. Sometimes a little tough love but, hmm, love nonetheless.

Now you know you can go quarter hogging or even less. Nothing is more important than showing up, at the gym or for that tough conversation. Showing up means you are mentally and emotionally prepared to make challenging changes. Showing up means you've already won your first round against fear. What other dragons do you need to slay?

Fear of Simon Cowell

A cocky *X factor* contestant arrives ready to impress the judges with their talent. They smash out a line or tune and one (or all) of the judges quickly signals for them to stop. And the bad-boy judge Simon Cowell, (usually) asks, 'What makes you think you can sing?' The contestant, stunned because they were expecting to be showered with praise, replies sulkily, 'My friends and family always tell me I can sing and I should go on this show'. To which Cowell says, 'Go home and tell them they're wrong'. Some contestants are crushed; others stomp out in a rage, declaring they'll come back bigger than Beyoncé. They seldom do, but it makes for great TV.

The judges often wonder on camera how some contestants have the gall to show up with no talent or training and without practising but full of misplaced confidence in their God-given gifts. It's all quite cringey and sad. The public humiliation, the lack of self-awareness and of course the false flattery by friends and family set them up to fail.

Perhaps you fear a Simon Cowell moment of your own. What if you suck when you try to be funny? Don't worry, that won't happen. You are in good hands. With this book I have only one agenda: to set you up for success. So, I'll deal out tough love when necessary and won't flatter you excessively as friends or family may do. (Mum, if you're reading this book, put it down now!)

You'll craft everything to suit your purpose, your audience, your message and most of all your personality. On this quest you will never chase after some half-baked idea or fly by the seat of your pants. You may worry you'll go off the rails with too much metaphorical glitter, too much sizzle and not enough steak. But there's something that will always ground us. Your audience and your wish to serve them are your north star. Please resume breathing now.

You will work with your strengths, and I will show you how to be authentic to who you are. Most of all, you'll do the work together in private with me before you show up in public with your presentation. This will prepare you, giving you both the permission and the confidence. So when you unleash your X factor, even Simon Cowell will be impressed.

Too early, too late?

The average age of an *X factor* winner is 24.1 years. Age comes up regularly on the show, but only if a contestant looks very young or much older than the median. Older contestants always intrigue the judges. They want to know where they've been their whole life and why they didn't break through earlier. Yup, this may be the last ageist show on the planet.

Maybe you're concerned about this too. Is it too early or too late in your career to make these moves? So let me be clear: **X factor is for early-career, mid-career, late-career, even post-career professionals. Get in early if you can, but it's never too late.** At 83, Japanese adventurer Kenichi Horie recently became the oldest person in the world to complete a solo non-stop voyage across the Pacific Ocean. He declares he is still 'in the middle of my youth' and 'not done yet'. Brilliant. That's the spirit. Horie for Mayor!

I get a lot of feedback from leaders all over the world sharing their regret. They wish they had discovered their X factor earlier. Please don't set up that obstacle. There's a popular Chinese proverb: The best time to plant a tree was 20 years ago. The second-best time is now. For growth and success, the best time to act is now.

You have X factor potential. Imagine You Unlimited. Your new future is waiting. Embrace these useful beliefs as you move forward.

CHAPTER 3

THE NEW MODEL

Mark T. Bertolini is CEO of Bridgewater Associates, one of the world's largest hedge funds. Bertolini says the biggest change he made in his time as leader was improving his mental heuristics, the mental models or shortcuts that allow us to solve problems and make judgements quickly and efficiently. How? Three ways: he improved the quality of his reading material, he reserved two nights a week to have dinner with people he didn't know, and he began learning about Eastern philosophy.

Time to apply this mindset and get familiar with some new heuristics: specifically, a new presentation model. You'll look at how X factor fits into this model and how you can apply X factor to the necessary but sometimes mundane aspects of a presentation. This is critical, because X factor isn't just something you sprinkle on top but is woven all the way through, if you know how. This work lifts your entire presentation.

POORNA

Let me introduce you to Poorna Malavath (also written as Malavath Poorna or Purna Malavath). She is only 10 years old and is getting ready to leave her tiny village in Telangana, South India. Her father wanted Poorna to get a better education and to experience life beyond their village, so he sends her off to school in the city of Secunderabad, almost 200 kilometres away. It's a government residential school that aims to educate underprivileged children.

Recalling her experience, Poorna shares how 'stepping out of my village gave me opportunities I didn't even dream of. In my new school, I felt like a newborn butterfly emerging from her cocoon'. In her new school Poorna enrolled in a mountain climbing workshop. At only 13 years and 11 months Poorna Malavath became the youngest Indian and the youngest female in the world to scale Mount Everest.

Since she climbed Everest the number of applications for admission at her school increased from 8,700 students to 60,000 a year. Poorna's story has inspired thousands upon thousands of children from disadvantaged backgrounds to believe that anything is possible.

Poorna, in Sanskrit, means fullness or whole. It's a principle she lives by wholeheartedly. Like other athletes, she knows her success depends on a holistic approach to training, mindset, health and nutrition. Before every climb she spends months training. She runs 20 kilometres every day and maintains a high-protein diet.

In the interests of *poorna*, wholeness put the rest of your presentation on steroids: it's X factored or Xed. This is important, because otherwise your shiny, dazzling X factor will make even a decent presentation look shabby in comparison. It's like renovating one room of a house. It looks amazing, but it makes the rest of the house look more rundown than it did before.

Poorna is also about congruence. When you lift the rest of your presentation, then your X factor, while still enchanting your audience, won't shock them. They don't scratch their heads, look at each other and ask, 'Now where did that come from? Must have read a bestselling book [*wink*]'.

I know you're probably champing at the bit and just want to get on with it. But this preliminary work won't delay your discovery of your X factor; in fact, it will make it easier to identify. This is all part of finding your X factor. Imagine the rewards that await. At the end of this chapter, you might have pulled together the rough, uncut X factor stones you can polish through the rest of the book. And your entire presentation is starting to dazzle.

THE NEW MODEL

Returning to Vinh Giang's model introduced in chapter 1, a presentation should comprise:

- 30% content
- 30% delivery
- 30% inspiration
- 10% X factor.

Economists are always pursuing the sweet spot between effectiveness and effort. Nothing expresses this better than the Pareto principle, which states that 20% of our efforts yield 80% of our results. I will now apply Pareto's law to each element of Vinh's model and give you tools that will provide you with an 80% lift, the strategies that offer the greatest impact, the most bang for your buck for content, delivery and inspiration. I will cover these three elements in this chapter. The rest of the book covers 10% X factor.

CONTENT XED

To X factor your content, you are going to learn how to *start with fire*, to craft sexy messages and finish with a bang.

Start with fire

When selling fire extinguishers, start with fire, goes an old adage. I often see charismatic leaders morph into boring ole' Clark Kent instead of Superman when they present. One way to channel Superman when presenting is to start strong. Why is this so important? Audiences are tough on poor starts. According to a recent Roy Morgan survey, 66% of respondents said they were unwilling to give someone who made a bad first impression a second chance. **You get one shot, so start with fire, not kryptonite.**

When I work with clients to rock their presentations, I suggest some of these starts:

- Ask a question that ties in with the topic that follows. At a recent conference, a speaker opened with, 'What stops you from achieving your full potential?' This question captured the attention of the audience, who were all eager to hear what followed.
- Use a story. Mellody Hobson is an investment expert. Her TED talk 'Color blind or color brave?' is on the subject of race. She begins her presentation with a personal story. She and a friend were attending an editorial board lunch in New York. They turn up

dressed in their best suits and the receptionist walks them through a series of corridors to a room and asks them 'where are your uniforms?'. As African Americans they had been mistaken for staff. The story is gobsmacking, engaging and persuasive. Hobson can almost rest her case there. There's a trick to the best story starts, and it's simple: Never start with window dressing like 'Before I start, I want to share a story ...' Aargh! That robs the story of its power. Remember, you are starting with fire. Plunge straight into the story, and once you have shared it, tie it back to the point you're making.

- Use a stat or data point — for example, 'One in three people will suffer from anxiety attacks in their lifetime'. Discipline yourself to use one piece of data that is big enough for your message to hang off. Don't use too many facts or too much data at the start, as that can leave your audience reeling.

Start with fire. Engage and inspire your audience. Hook them and have them leaning in for more.

Sexy messages

A presentation should have one, three or five key messages. Anymore and your audience won't remember them. Key messages are what you want your audience to understand, remember and take away from your presentation. Once you have identified your key messages, dress them up and make them sexy, by which I mean package them into memorable and repeatable soundbites. This is not about dumbing down your messages but *smartening* them so people will connect and remember.

The first way to make your key messages sexy is to *find the right words* to convey them, words that are memorable and grab people's attention. Lim, a client, had two key messages to convey to his team: 'results from last year', which were outstanding and 'targets for this year'. Stock communications, but he made them sexy by calling his first message 'Why I love you' and the second 'Why you fear me'. He began his presentation by saying, 'I want to start by telling you why I love you'. *Kaboom!* He has everyone's attention. Compare that with a more conventional, 'I'm here to share last year's results'.

The second way is to put a spin on a conventional message. What if you have a boring message that has already been said? Your challenge in sexing it up is to put a spin on it. Consider the titles of some hugely influential books.

In 2001, Jim Collins hit the bestseller list with *Good to Great*, in which he offers timeless insights into management techniques and practice. In 2011 Simon Sinek turned the corporate world upside down with *Start with Why*, an inspirational bestseller that asked us to focus on our purpose and motivation and ignited a movement. Dr Brené Brown changed the leadership landscape forever with a string of inspirational bestsellers. Her 2018 book *Dare to Lead: Brave Work, Tough Conversations, Whole Hearts* taught us how to step up into brave leadership.

Think of the allure and promise of these titles. They are sexy! That's what you want. Key messages presented with chutzpah and flair to excite and enthral your audience.

Finally, your sexy message must be short, 15 to 30 seconds maximum.

Finish with a bang

In June 2021, along with two close friends, I organised a fundraising lunch for Covid relief in India. We decided to cook and share authentic, regional, traditional Indian food. This is the food you would eat if you were invited into a private home in Chennai, Tamil Nadu, South India. We came up with a mouth-watering menu, with not a nan or butter chicken in sight. The response was overwhelming, and the lunch was booked out in hours. Then the enormity of it all hit us. While all three of us are good home cooks, and we had a wonderful army of volunteers at hand, none of us had hospitality experience on this kind of scale and service.

Then, as if by magic, appeared the amazing Loki Madireddi, MasterChef Australia finalist (2018). Loki generously volunteered his time, skills and expertise. One thing he said really stuck with me. He said your first course should be exquisite. If this first impression is off the charts, then everything that follows is valued. Equally important, is the last course you serve, dessert should be a feast for the eyes and a taste of heaven in your mouth. Not everyone, however, eats dessert (who are these people?) and some people leave early and miss out on dessert.

Loki applies the laws of primacy and recency to the dining experience. What people hear, see or eat first and last is what they best remember. Now, you have a couple of choices about how you finish your presentation. You can just let it peter out, like fizz leaving uncorked champagne, or you can finish with a bang. When you finish with a bang, people who made the mistake of leaving early hear so much about this ending that they deeply regret missing your fabulous finish because they had to rush off to that important meeting. And no one will ever make the grave mistake of leaving your presentations early again!

Let's apply the law of recency. What are you going to leave your audience with? You could give a summary, then launch your power ending:

- Share a quote.
- Give a call to action.
- Share a story that wraps it all up.

Your turn. How are you going to finish your presentation? What's the last thing you want to say? Next, I'll look at delivery, and how you can create emotion, personalise and embrace a beta mindset.

DELIVERY XED

Three million players and counting
Most begin their day with it
The internet goes into meltdown over it

A confession. My name is Yamini and I'm a Wordle addict! Wordle isn't the only, the earliest or even the best word game, so what explains its phenomenal success? Well, its origin story is based on love: the founder created it for his word puzzle-loving partner. But the love doesn't stop there.

Wordle seems to be built on love for the user, which is not a business, tech or social media trope we're familiar with. A simple ad-free website, no email logins or passwords, no app to download — pure user nirvana. Wordle also protects us from ourselves. It provides only one game per day; six guesses and you're done. You can't binge even if you wanted to. A refreshing contrast to tech that sets its hooks and tries to keep you addicted for as long as possible. It's a single-user game, but you can share both your results and the experience with others. A small spark of joy in the daily grind. What's not to love about the user experience?

As a presenter you have much the same challenge. There's little point in having the best content if it's poorly delivered. Delivery is about one thing and one thing only: the audience experience you create. And the first key to creating an experience through your delivery is personalisation. This is often overlooked or underestimated by presenters.

Hello, is it me you're looking for?

Live performers will often open their performance by saying, 'Hello, [city name]'.

Performers know the power of personalisation. This simple opening works, making their audience feel special and honoured.

And the wrath of an audience when they get this wrong knows no bounds. In their 2017 tour of Australia, Guns N' Roses announcer shouted 'Sydney' just before the band entered the stage in Melbourne. The Melbourne audience immediately started booing. What made this worse is the deep-seated historic rivalry between the two cities. To confuse them outraged the audience. The band quickly took to social media to apologise: 'Melbourne! Accidentally after 30 years McBob made an error, we're truly sorry. Thank you for coming out tonight!' The fans forgave them, one replying to the post, 'One mistake every 30 years … Reasonable'.

Personalisation sounds simple, but you can't afford to get it wrong, even if you are a legendary rock band with an adoring fan base.

What are some simple ways you can personalise your presentation? Use names, including your client's company name. Use examples relevant to the audience, but always weave in their names. This is so much easier online as usually everyone enters with their name displaying on the screen, unless they have changed their name to DonkeyKong'81. *Hmm*, you might think, *I see we have an arcade platform video game fan here*. Of course, if that's really their name, then you're on your own, and no amount of knowledge about early Nintendo games will dig you out of this hole.

Small things make a big difference. Experience strategist and former head of VIP events at Cirque du Soleil, Carolene Méli, sees personalisation as a powerhouse as it creates connection and a sense of belonging. Méli says, '**The best events make you feel you were meant to be there.**' Personalisation makes your presentation memorable and worth sharing.

Tasting stars

When French Benedictine monk, Dom Pérignon, invented champagne in the 17th century, the story goes, he shouted to his fellow monks, 'Come quick, I'm tasting stars!' Irresistible. What powers your delivery and gives it star power is *emotion*. Think back to a recent memorable experience you've had, perhaps a family holiday, a visit to the farmers market or a beach walk. How did it make you feel? Maya Angelou once said, 'I've learned that people will forget what you said, people will forget what you did, but people will never forget how you made them feel'.

Emotion breathes life into your presentation. Without emotion, any presentation will flatline. Emotion helps you surprise and delight your audience.

Most presentations are about telling, communicating information and using strategies like sexy messaging to hold your audience's attention. But you can't stay in telling mode for your entire presentation or it won't be a presentation so much as a monologue.

So how can you move out of telling? Think of the writer's technique *show don't tell*. You can show your point through an anecdote, a story or a metaphor. Start small with an example; it's like tying your shoelaces, like taking a train. Examples help clarify a point. They are sort of halfway between a metaphor and a story. Show don't tell with props. Underused in business, props can make an abstract point concrete. Obviously, you don't want to haul in a grand piano, so use your props appropriately, again only if they add value.

Show don't tell by sharing a video or something unusual. When Jill Bolte Taylor was presenting a talk about her stroke she entered the stage carrying a large plastic brain. Online I use custom-made signs (printed on A3 paper and laminated) for my audience. These include fun signs like 'Mild laughter', 'Wild laughter' and 'Joke didn't land'. The last one gets the biggest laugh! For one of your messages, after you share your message, consider how you can you *show* your audience the message?

Another way to create emotion is through involving your audience all the way through your presentation. Ways to do this can be as simple as asking for a show of hands or inviting them to discuss something in pairs. In a virtual session, place people in breakout rooms, ask them to pop something in chat or unmute. You can also ask for any questions, comments or observations. This way you give your audience a choice and are much more likely to get a response.

Two of the most powerful ways to invoke emotion in your presentation are to use humour and storytelling. I'll return to these when we look at inspiration shortly.

Embrace beta

The last key for delivery is mindset. Recently people on the 'open mic' comedy circuit (which is free for audiences and performers) were surprised to see Dave Hughes step up. Hughes is a huge Australian comedy star with his own radio and TV shows. Yet there he was, doing the hard yards, cheek by jowl with people trying to break into the business. Hughes was demonstrating what all good comedians do: they embrace a beta mindset. They constantly practise and road test their material. **A beta mindset learns from both the bombs and the bouquets.**

Practise before every session. Practise alone and aloud and record it on your phone. A key secret shared by many professional speakers is to record each presentation and review it later to see what they could do better or differently, what worked and what didn't. **The road from amateur to professional is paved with practice.**

Next, I'll look at inspiration, and how you can use storytelling and humour.

INSPIRATION XED

The *Collins Dictionary* informs us that inspiration is 'a feeling of enthusiasm you get from someone or something, which gives you new and creative ideas'. Sometimes you watch a speaker deliver an inspiring presentation and wish that was you up there. And it could be, if you know how. Inspiration is not an exclusive club reserved for a select few.

Two tools that every professional speaker learns are storytelling and humour and, yes, both can be taught and learned. As a professional speaker, I can tell you that we live by the motto: you don't have to share stories or be funny, unless you want to be paid.

Storytelling

As tennis players swing rackets and rock stars trash hotel rooms, speakers share stories. I have written several books on storytelling, including a bestseller. That's because storytelling in the business context is a big topic. You must learn how to tell stories and if you don't already know how, my book *Story Mastery: How leaders supercharge results with storytelling* should be your first port of call (once you've finished this book, of course). For now, here's storytelling Xed, and some fast and furious tips just for you.

Leaders often ask me, 'How do we use business storytelling effectively in our presentations?' Smart, successful professionals know stories can make or break a presentation. What makes some stories better than others and some storytellers more successful than others? The answers might surprise you.

Make a point

How do you fix an air leak on board the International Space Station when you don't even know where the leak is? Cosmonaut Anatoly Ivanishin carefully tore open a tea bag and watched the tea leaves as they floated in microgravity towards a scratch in the wall through which air had been escaping. The crew then patched the hole up with sticky tape. At work as in life, not every solution has to be whiz-bang. Ivanishin's ingenious idea illustrates how sometimes a simple solution will do just fine.

It's important that every story you share links to your message, otherwise you are wasting your audience's time by being self-indulgent. **Your stories are there to help your audience connect and remember your messages, so use them purposefully.**

Make it personal

A client recently highlighted how one of his CEOs used to share stories about Jack Welch and GE. And the minute either of these topics was mentioned, everyone would roll their eyes, thinking, here we go again. Sadly, that CEO (who didn't last long in the role) interpreted business storytelling literally, as meaning stories about business.

Business storytelling is about humanising us, allowing us to make an H2H (human-to-human) connection at work. There's no simpler yet more powerful way to do this than through personal stories. You can occasionally use business stories, but successful storytellers know to always go personal.

Small beats big

In business storytelling, David beats Goliath every time. Often my clients put themselves under pressure, thinking their stories must be mega — on scaling Everest or sailing solo around the world. When products or brands are the themes, presenters often share the entire brand history, rather than focusing on individual customer experiences. But what works best is small, everyday, relatable stories. Stories about shopping in your local supermarket or going to a restaurant with friends or dropping your kids off at school. In a world in which bigger is better, brash is bought and bold is rewarded, this is a hard truth to face. In storytelling, every time you go personal, small and intimate you set yourself up for success.

Compare a story that begins with 'In airports around the world, people ...' with one that begins with 'At Melbourne airport this morning, I ...' Everyday stories work because your audience can relate to them. They see themselves in your stories. They relive their experiences through your story, and nothing is more powerful than that.

Stakes matter

Even in a small, everyday, relatable story something must be at stake. Your reputation or integrity? Your career? While it may have felt important to you at the time, a story about a barista not making your morning coffee right won't engage your audience, because they don't have a stake in it. Some will dismiss it as a first-world problem and you as a privileged twat. Think of a story that starts with driving your child to school (most people can relate to this), and during the ride you learn that they are being bullied. Suddenly the stakes are high and your audience is engaged. High stakes mean you are sharing something important, something that matters deeply to you, and this will make it matter to your audience too.

Trust me

For *Seinfeld*'s George Costanza, 'It's not a lie if you believe it'! The opposite applies in business storytelling. For your storytelling to be successful, everything about it needs to be authentic.

Your stories need to be both factually and authentically true. You, the storyteller, need to believe in your story and its purpose. Your intent needs to be authentic. A few years ago, I did some work with a leadership team that was outsourcing some of their work overseas and they were looking for stories to accompany it. When none emerged, I asked them, 'Can you put your hand on your heart and say you believe this is the best thing for your company?' And they couldn't. Unless you believe in its purpose, your story will not be authentic. But please don't strip out all the fun from your story either.

The second tool for inspiration is humour. Here are some tips you can begin to apply immediately even if you think you are not funny.

Humour

In her bestseller *Holy Cow: An Indian Adventure*, former ABC journalist Sarah Macdonald shares her magical and madcap adventures in India. She tells a story about attending a 10-day Vipassana retreat, a residential program in which the guru and founder teaches meditation but the entire retreat is held in silence. Every day the participants watched videos of the founder teaching and practising. Midway through the 10 days, Sarah and the other participants were watching a video when someone accidentally pressed fast forward. And there was their revered guru comically sped up. Everyone burst out into uncontrollable laughter, rolling on the ground, wiping tears from their eyes.

You might have raised an eyebrow reading this and thought, hmm, it's not that funny. Well, no, it's not, but I'm sharing it with you to make the point that with humour, context matters and the bar is generally low. In the Vipassana course, participants had been silent for so long that the smallest stimulus was enough to provoke a powerful response.

The good news is that in business, too, the bar is low. You need to provide only the slightest stimulus to generate a tsunami of laughter. Yet when you think of being funny in a presentation, you may imagine you need to be as consistently funny as a seasoned comedian. Of course, comedians work on it full time and get paid to make strangers laugh. 'It's never too late to start exercising,' says Ellen DeGeneres. 'My grandma started walking five miles a day when she was 60. She's 97 today, and we have no idea where she is.' Ellen is a professional and probably has a team of writers. Right in the middle between *ho hum* (which is most of business communication and presentations) and *hilarious* lies the ground you must claim. Actually you need to move the dial only a little to be joyful, uplifting and funny. **Laughter lowers the drawbridge to your audience's heart.**

First, some important groundwork before you can X factor your humour. Traditional humour is dad jokes. Here's one: Did you hear about the restaurant on the moon? Great food, no atmosphere. Or even worse: How many apples grow on a tree? All of them.

Let's put an end to that crime right here and now. Can I get you (whether you are a dad or not) to hold up your right hand and declare, 'When I'm at work I solemnly swear I will tell no more dad jokes'. A pat on the back and it's safe to proceed. Let's learn some way to add humour or at least some light-heartedness to your presentations.

It all begins with a smile.

Smile

You can't pour from an empty cup. To use humour as a presenter, you must present with a sense of light-heartedness, a smile on your lips. I know your topic can sometimes be serious. But some presenters walk in as if the entire weight of the world presses down on their shoulders. If you present this way, it makes the audience feel heavy, gloomy, like they're sinking into the ground, even before you have spoken a word.

What about those days when you can barely drag yourself out of bed in the morning? Even faking a smile floods your body with endorphins, raises the dopamine levels in your brain and leaves you feeling happier. Try it now, don't take my word for it. Do a few fake smiles. Feel better already?

Funny file

You don't have to dream up humour from scratch; you can curate it. Start collecting funny quotes, funny stories and amusing customer questions. Look around you. See a funny sign? Take a photo and use it in your next presentation.

To paraphrase one of our public safety announcements ('Be alert, not alarmed'): 'Be funny alert all the time'. I was flying Qantas one Friday evening, a business flight home. You probably know the feeling well — that last flight home, packed with grumpy business travellers. Everyone just wants to get home. A crew member was making the standard safety announcements before take-off. He said, 'We are going to dim the cabin lights for take-off and because it's more flattering for our crew'. Everyone laughed, and some people even cheered! I immediately whipped out my phone and 'funny filed' the incident.

Channel your inner boy scout

Our only guarantee in life, beyond death and taxes, is that things will go wrong. Murphy's law. It's hard to think of a humorous quip on the spot when things go wrong on stage, but like a boy scout you can be prepared. For example, technology will usually fail at some point. Can you prepare a funny line to use should this happen? When I ask for questions and don't get an immediate response, I might say, 'Let's ask Siri. "Hey Siri, any questions?" And Siri's response: "That's my line"!'

Sally Hogshead, author of *Fascinate*, shares this example: 'The moment I walked on stage for a recent speech, my microphone died. I said: "Don't worry, I've been trained in mime … and I'll be delivering the entire speech in interpretive dance".' By the time the laughter died down, my new mic was ready to go, and the speech went on to a standing ovation.'

Savers

You need a funny in your pocket for when your audience doesn't laugh. This is called a 'saver line'. Mine is to use the organiser's name and say with a smile, 'Jane, this is a tough crowd'. Even if you don't have a saver line, it's important to smile to yourself and move on quickly. Don't let them see your disappointment … or panic. Just give a bit of a nod that you have amused yourself and model the behaviour you're encouraging.

Number one rule: keep going. The show must go on. If you're mortified that they didn't laugh, don't let it show on your face. A smile is your best friend. So smile and keep going. Like Dory, in *Finding Nemo*, just keep swimming, just keep swimming. And just keep smiling, just keep smiling.

Work with a mentor

A few years ago, I debuted as a stand-up comedian. I'm being generous in using the word 'debut', as it was a very humble sort of start. While my street cred skyrocketed, why I chose to do it intrigues people. **The truth is stand-up comedy is simply the best personal and professional development you can pursue as a presenter.**

The more I learn about the art and science of comedy, the more I realise this is possibly one of the hardest skills on the planet to master. Yes, *science*. Renowned Japanese theoretical physicist Michio Kau features in a BBC documentary series called *Time,* exploring the properties and challenges of time. In the very first episode he looks at the science of the link between good timing and successful comedy.

But before I smash the tender yearning that was blossoming in your wee heart, here's a gigantic ball of hope for all of us. Humour can be taught and learned, and you can get better at it.

For several years I have worked on humour with a paid mentor. That's why I'm good. (And modest!) And if I'm not, you now know where to direct customer complaints. This is the most important tip I can give you: If you're serious about using humour at work and want to learn fast and accelerate your progress, work with a mentor. Two of the best in the business are Robbi Mack, CSP (www.robbimack.com), and Kate Burr (www.kateburr.com). I have worked with both and can't recommend them too highly. Please know that this is a genuine heartfelt recommendation, not some shonky affiliation link or paid promotion.

NON, JE NE REGRETTE RIEN

Reading all this, you might think, whoa, that's a lot of work to X content, delivery and inspiration, even though I have given you the best tips to speed this up by channelling the *Fast and Furious* movies, all nine of them.

While writing this chapter, I've been playing Édith Piaf in the background, especially her signature song 'Non, je ne regrette rien'. No, I regret nothing. 'Je ne regrette rien' was Piaf's biggest hit and her legacy. But it is unlikely that

Piaf herself would have felt this way towards the end of her life. Years of alcohol abuse, over-medication and a stormy personal life took their toll. Piaf died at age 47, a few years after the song was released. Her last words: 'Every damn thing you do in this life, you have to pay for'.

Wise words, but the reverse is also true. If you put in the work, you reap the rewards. Put this chapter into action; you will never regret Xing your presentation.

The last word must go to the hero you met at the start of this chapter, Poorna. At her book launch (there's nothing she can't do) students wanted to understand how to get started on a task that seems insurmountable. Simple, responded Poorna. 'Taking the first step is the best way to overcome your fear and march towards your goal'.

So now that you have established strong foundations, the 90% of your presentation, you are ready to move forward. Next, in Part B, I will help you explore multiple possibilities and experiment to find your X factor, the remaining 10%. Your future beckons.

PART B
DISCOVERING YOUR X FACTOR

CHAPTER 4

QUEST AHOY

You are sitting on a treasure chest of life experiences that together we will gently unpack to discover your X factor. To do this, you will set off on a quest to explore your heritage and history, hobbies and passions, even your quirks. You have a world of possibilities before you. You'll trigger a space-time ripple by time travelling to your past and your future.

For any quest to be successful, there must be lots of preparation, poring over maps, packing supplies, creating a plan (even a rough one), sharpening tools (evil laughter optional) and anticipating the potential dangers ahead.

For the best outcomes, approach these preparations with kindness, non-judgementally (wherever possible), open to both what might come up for you and what is available to you. I find clients who are open to all possibilities find their X factor faster.

Opening up to find your X factor is rewarding. Kick vanilla (in presentations, not ice-cream flavour) to the kerb, sign a death warrant for the beige brigade right here and now. Start by being kind to yourself, as this makes finding your X factor easier and more fun.

THE TOUGHEST RULE

In my workshops, I have three rules of engagement:

1. Be kind to yourself.
2. Be kind to others. As author Damian Barr says, 'We are not all in the same boat. We are all in the same storm. Some of us are on super-yachts. Some have just the one oar'.
3. Have some fun. The best learning happens when people are having fun.

The first rule in my workshops, be kind to yourself, is often the toughest to absorb. Achievement and self-compassion can feel at odds. But TED speaker and psychologist Susan David explains, 'Self-compassionate people aim just as high as self-critical people do. The difference is that self-compassionate people don't fall apart when goals are not met'.

So, to find your X factor start by being kind to yourself through self-compassion. Self-compassion sharpens your edge. It is associated with healthy behaviours like eating right, exercising and managing stress through tough times when you must care for yourself the most. To rework a popular maxim, when the going gets tough, the tough get self-compassionate. The emerging field of self-compassion research is producing some clear results: it turns out that being kind to yourself is key to successful learning as well as to your long-term physical and mental health.

Remember, your X factor doesn't have to be BIG, unless you're a Cirque du Soleil performer (don't create that pressure for yourself). The X factor in your work can be as simple as being empathetic and courteous. For example, New Zealand Prime Minister Jacinda Ardern is enormously popular because she connects in a way that is down-to-earth and relatable. That's her X factor.

How can you practise self-compassion, the deepest form of self-care, daily? For me, most days I meditate, write in a reflection journal, try to be wholly present when connecting with family and friends, and spend time in nature. I am still learning to accept compliments (feel free) and to be less hard on myself for any mistakes.

Why is self-compassion essential to discovering your X factor?

You practise kindness and grace because your X factor won't emerge from your prefrontal cortex, from conscious verbal thinking. What? So where then? It will emerge from the 'Three Wise I's'. But before we go there, here's a quest checklist for self-compassion. These are micro actions I invite you to take. Don't be deceived by the word micro. As storyteller and artist Danielle Doby puts it in her book *I Am Her Tribe*, 'No act is ever too small. One by one, this is how to make an ocean rise'.

Quest checklist

- Find a 'sit spot'. Author Claire Dunn describes this as a place in nature that calls to you. Perhaps it's a hidden spot in a city park or in your backyard, or somewhere close to home that feels good. Seek it out and immerse yourself in it regularly — Dunn recommends daily.
- Allow yourself to do one thing you love every day.
- Write yourself a fan letter describing what you love about yourself.
- Start every day by giving yourself three love bombs: tell yourself three things you love about yourself.
- Take regular mental health days off.

THE 'THREE WISE I'S' — INSIGHT, INSTINCT AND INTUITION

When my dear friend and yoga teacher Kanchana Rao was pregnant with her first child, she met His Holiness the Dalai Lama, the Buddhist teacher and leader. She asked him how she could be a good mother. He laughed with his wonderful childlike abandon. 'Does a cow need to learn how to look after her calf? It's already in you, just be natural!' So much is, yet some of us are reluctant to trust our deepest instincts and knowledge.

Your X factor is primal. It comes from your gut; it's probably already living there. That's good news. It will emerge through your insight, instinct or intuition, the three wise I's. Here we can tap into the ancient indigenous wisdom of Australia and practise Dadirri or deep listening. Aboriginal writer and senior elder Miriam-Rose Ungunmerr-Baumann describes it like this: 'Dadirri is inner, deep listening and quiet, still awareness. Dadirri recognises the deep spring that is inside us. We call on it and it calls to us ... It is something like what we call contemplation'.

To find your X factor using your insight, instinct and intuition, you need to move from *knowing* and *doing* to *being* and *feeling*. **Your X factor will unfold from your gut, like a much-anticipated gift from someone who knows you well.** It can feel like a niggle that won't go away. Gradually, over time, the message will break through into your rational mind until suddenly you find you can easily describe and verbalise your special brand of magic.

For a professional, *being* and *feeling* can be hard concepts to contend with. If someone had brought them to my attention a few years ago, my response would probably have been cynical or maybe openly mocking. I know, sorry, not very nice. Business is all about hustle, so such heart-based advice used to go down like a lead balloon. So, wait and navel gaze until something happens? Absolutely not. Think of it like this: Pilots rely on their instruments, sight — what they can see from the cockpit, and their instinct. (If you are a nervous flyer, note in bad weather, pilots fly with their instruments). You will do the same. This is the instinct part, so fasten your seatbelt and seal the exits.

Trusting your instincts takes courage and sometimes means bucking conventional advice. *In a white room, a white skeleton appears that tries to catch me, then instantly everything around me becomes white.* This was how Hergé, creator of *The Adventures of Tintin*, described a recurring nightmare to a psychiatrist. The psychiatrist, concerned, advised him to retire, but Hergé disregarded the advice. He was struggling with writer's block at the time, so he dealt with it by channelling his nightmare onto a blank page. He drew Tintin in white sheets roaming, lost in snow, and another bestseller was born, *Tintin in Tibet*. Hergé knew to go with his instinct, rather than repressing it. If he hadn't, this bestseller, his twentieth book, and the books that followed it would never have been written. *Billions of bilious blue blistering barnacles*, as Captain Haddock would say.

I love Bollywood dancing (and all dance), but I had never thought of it as special enough to qualify as a potential X factor candidate. I have trained in various dance forms and have often performed in amateur dance crews, but I've never danced professionally. In my head, I set up all these barriers. Once I saw Bollywood dance being attempted on stage by a large, sweaty, breathless presenter. It was pure cringe and a giant turn-off. I took what was almost a blood oath there and then that that would never be me.

Yet every time I did a bit of Bollywood at a conference, usually as an energiser, it would be the talk of the event. The conference organisers would feature it in a highlights reel. Who doesn't like guaranteed footage of people laughing and having a wild time? The audience would write about it in their reviews ('Loved the Bollywood! Such fun. More please!') and delegates would tell me how much they enjoyed it and wished it had lasted longer. Some even wanted to know where they could learn it.

Even though the world was banging on my door, sending an emergency vehicle with sirens blaring to give me the news, I remained hesitant. I kept on denying my instincts and looking outside myself for something else. There is a saying in Hindi that translates as 'chicken cooked at home tastes like lentils'. If something feels too familiar, too easy, too natural, you can dismiss it.

While the three wise I's are important, we don't follow our every instinct blindly. In the following chapters, you will road test each of your instinctive candidates and pick only your stars.

Time for some micro actions to help you find your three wise I's.

Quest checklist

- Practise stopping and taking three deep breaths throughout your day.
- Teach yourself to meditate, even if only for five minutes a day.
- Create an awesome feedback folder. Every complimentary message, email or note you receive goes in there. Scour your memory for compliments and add these to your folder.
- List all the times you have presented and had a positive result: you won the pitch, the client signed up or you were complimented by your boss.

- Add to a reflection notebook after every presentation.
- Start recording your presentations. Be a hero and do it. Nothing provides more opportunities for learning than this single step.
- What's your party trick? Maybe you can wiggle your ears or do a nifty card trick or do complex fractions in your head. Note it down.

CAUTION, FRACTIONS

A newish speaker who heard me talk about X factor said he thought he would be ready in another five years' time. But why wait? What stopped him from starting right away? He said, 'But I've nothing to start with!' The solution is simple: start small and where you are at right now. A maths teacher hangs a 'Caution, fractions' warning outside his door instead of a standard 'Do not disturb' sign. That's a tiny X factor right there.

This grace allows you to start with what you know best and build on it. In 2011, Tal Winter and Kate Cutler, two best friends, launched bkr (pronounced *beaker*) with a focus on 'Beauty 101: drinking water is the foundation for soft, dewy, pretty skin — and wtf — hydrating shouldn't be so hard'. All they knew when they started was that they wanted the water bottles they created to be glass. It took time to produce a prototype they liked. The water bottles are now small-mouthed, original, sustainable and eco-friendly. Each bottle has a silicone sleeve, which is a signature element, and they infuse each bottle with personality. Bkr has attained cult-like status with the humble water bottle. And now they have nailed it again by adding another detail: perfect slim, water bottle–shaped ice cube trays.

Start small and where you are because, much as you might want it to, your X factor is seldom going to appear in one lightbulb moment. You might see yourself jumping out of your bathtub, shouting 'Eureka'. A lush, soft white towel wrapped around your body, you race through the streets, proudly holding up your X factor (which has magically morphed into a gold, Oscar-like statue) in one hand as your other hand clasps the towel, for modesty's sake ... and so you don't get arrested by any officer of the law who might take a different view of your revelation. The last rays of the sun cast you in a golden hue. People hold up their phones, clicking this vision of beauty and grace, and say to each other, 'Ahh, yet another person who found their X factor in the bathtub' ... Sadly, this glorious vision is just that — a mirage. To quote Darryl Kerrigan from the 1997 comedy film *The Castle*, 'Tell 'em they're dreaming'.

Give yourself permission to start small, to start where you are at right now, to allow your X factor to reveal itself gradually, and savour the process.

In yoga you can enjoy the benefits of inversion by doing a free headstand. Or, get this, simply lean your legs up against the wall. Robert Saper, MD, MPH, Chair of Wellness and Preventive Medicine at the Cleveland Clinic, says, 'The advantage of legs up the wall rather than a free headstand or shoulder stand is that you can achieve the benefits of inversion without stressing or straining your neck and head'. The. Same. Benefits. Again, start where you are to reap instant rewards.

Quest checklist

- Write one small change you can make to your next presentation.
- Could you use a physical prop, show a personal photo, share a brief anecdote?
- Don't make this hard; reach for easy opportunities here. Remember, you're building your X factor in small steps.

GUARD RAILS

The richness of your X factor hinges on your lived experiences at work and in your personal life. To find the pot of bitcoins at the end of the rainbow, you must explore the broad canvas of your own life. It is important to do this in a safe way.

I recognise that some parts of the work you will be doing in the following chapters (like delving into family, personal history and heritage) could bring back past traumatic memories for some. Psychologists and counsellors use the term 'triggering' when describing this experience. I have been very mindful of internal triggers when designing the exercises you will be doing. The most important thing is to keep yourself safe, so if you feel any exercises might carry this risk, you may choose to skip the exercise completely, do your own version of it or seek help. Do what you need to do to stay safe and protect your mental health.

Please note, though, that being triggered differs from being made to feel uncomfortable. If the work makes you feel uncomfortable, I invite you to sit with that feeling. It might be an early sign of a breakthrough. While I'm very proud of my heritage, at first I was uncomfortable about showcasing it on stage. It took time and perseverance to work through those feelings, and this book is a proud product of that journey.

On your X factor quest when you accidentally stray from the personal into the private, you might worry about oversharing. As always, it depends on who you are sharing with. Be careful about what you share and don't share. You get to choose what parts of your life are closed off by the guardrail of privacy. It's important to differentiate between personal (what you are happy to share) and private (what you choose not to share). In figure 4.1 each circle represents a different layer of access, from public to private. Only you can decide how much information you are comfortable to share in each layer.

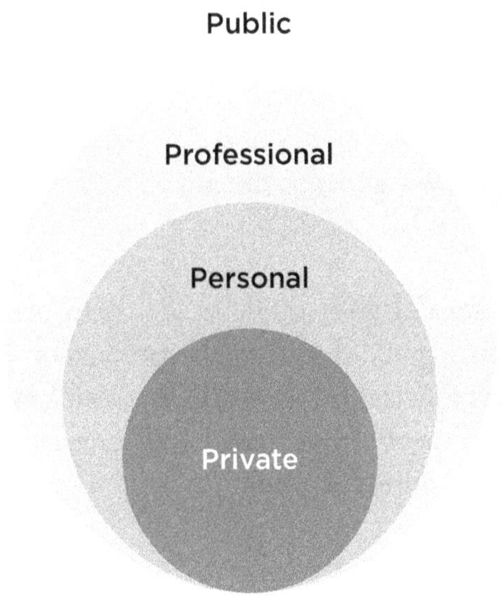

Figure 4.1 Public to private

The way I do Bollywood dancing at weddings or parties with friends and families is wild and uninhibited. Often one of us will do a total buffoon version of a step. It's mad and fun, like an 'in joke' for those of us who know. This is NOT the way I would dance for my clients. There I marry one step at a time with some content. I take my audience through a practice run, first without music and then with music. It's still a lot of fun and authentic, but it's the public version of my X factor.

You can probably trust yourself not to reveal more than you should, unless alcohol is involved! Finding your X factor is not like negotiating an obstacle course where an alarm goes off every time you make a mistake and a burly official escorts you back to the start.

Quest checklist

- Understand your triggers, choose the exercises wisely and seek help if you need it.
- Differentiate between being uncomfortable and being triggered.
- Look at the public vs private model and decide what you will and won't share.

You have started your quest in less than obvious places, from practising grace through self-compassion and trusting your instincts to welcoming small starts and learning how to take care of yourself. Now, like a well-prepared adventurer, plunge forth to mine for gold!

CHAPTER 5

MINING FOR GOLD

Time to channel *The Lion King*: 'Everything the light touches is mine!' To find your X factor you explore, inquire and invite. You mine for gold. You make a deep (riveting and exciting) dive into you. The many tools you will use are like paints on a palette. You look at them individually first so you can blend the colours into your X factor statement.

While it is a finite set of tools, the possible combinations are limitless. I've done these exercises with thousands of clients, and no one has ever ended up with the same combination. Not even one set of identical twins. This work is life changing. Let's start by looking at some golden tips for X factor discovery.

THE MAGIC OF DISCOVERY

Discovering your X factor is both a process (there are steps you can follow) and an art. You are smart, so your fierce, analytical, solutions-driven business brain may want a neat answer or set of answers and want them early. When this does not happen, resistance may show up in different guises. One is drifting down into your business self. Reaching out for the comfort of the familiar, for business jargon, your work role, your title. This is the single biggest reason for when and why the process breaks down and fails you.

The exercises in this chapter and this book are deep work, which can be challenging. Don't be too literal with how you do the exercises. Be open to possibilities and lateral in your approach. But please don't give in to the temptation to relapse into your business self. Here are other golden tips that set your X factor discovery up for success.

Go personal

My process unearths what lights you up, what sits below the surface, what sets your soul on fire? Thinking only with your business hat on is limiting. **The best, richest X factors emerge, not from business, but from your personal life.** You can then apply your X factor in a business context, but looking for your X factor only from your business life is too restricting.

Shortcut ban

While you're going through the process, don't take a shortcut and jump to early conclusions about what your X factor might be. Don't be like the hasty quiz contestant who hits their buzzer before the quiz master has completed the question and who then kicks themselves when their impatience costs them the prize.

Cast a wide net

Instead of chasing one idea single-mindedly, the process invites you to think about and work on a cluster of ideas, to cast a wide net. Pursuing only one idea reduces your chances of finding your X factor to almost nil. I won't sugar-coat this hard truth.

Fortune telling forbidden

While appearing simple, the process ahead is rich. Trying to predict the outcomes, for you or anyone else, is like fortune telling or mind reading. Instead of seizing on early conclusions or preconceived ideas I invite you to challenge your thinking through the exercises, to ask questions and think about your answers from different perspectives.

No end in mind

Conventionally in business, you 'start with the end in mind'. This is one of the habits from Stephen R. Covey's bestselling book *The 7 Habits of Highly Effective People*. But finding your X factor demands you buck this convention. In my experience the client who sets out with a word in mind that they want to feature in their X factor statement ends up with the weakest statement or no statement. It is like setting off on a race with blinkers on. You will fall or fail. Don't try to force fit words that you are wedded to. Time to gently let these words go, take a deep breath and proceed.

This is sounding like a lot of work. Why is it necessary? Pinning X factor down can feel like trying to nail jelly to a tree. Have you ever tried that? Possibly not. Personally, I love jelly (especially pink, raspberry flavour) too much to waste it! What would you think Oprah's X factor is? She is empathetic, a charismatic interviewer, very open about her life, relatable yet aspirational, someone who connects deeply with her audience. Her X factor is multifaceted, as is true of everyone — Oprah, you, your neighbour.

What makes X factor hard to grasp is that it lives in multiplicity. It is never one thing, but a mix of many things. Multiple elements, like your talents, skills, hobbies, passions, life experiences, your heritage, your history and your quirks, inform your X factor. This is good news. Never pin your hopes on one big thing. Instead, look for your X factor in a special mix of things. To help you get there fast I have distilled the process into three vital steps. Welcome to the 3X Super Steps.

3X SUPER STEPS

The 3X Super Steps are:

1. **Gather.** Gather field data from your personal life and use to inform and shape your X factor statement.
2. **Zing.** Learn how to make this data 'zing', through the magic of words and interlinking circles.
3. **Craft.** Use several tools to craft and recraft your X factor statement.

Even if tempted, don't skip any of these steps. Following each step guarantees an X factor that is rich, distinctive and desirable. You need this range and depth to capture your X factor.

The three steps are detailed but not difficult. In *The Big Bang Theory*, Sheldon creates a long list of complicated rules for a game called Rock Paper Scissors Lizard Spock. Our 3X Super Steps are the opposite of that. They are simple to follow but you need to work on them because your X factor lives in multiplicity.

Go to **xfactor.yamininaidu.com.au** or scan this QR code and download the 3X Super Steps template now. It is also available at the end of this book under 'Additional Resources'.

I recommend you fill in the template using pen and paper. Neuroscience research shows that handwriting opens different neural pathways in our brain. Trust me, analogue works best here. But *please carefully read the very important caution below before filling out the template.*

So, what do you do?

When asked what you do for work, what do you say? I say I'm an author, educator and speaker. This combination brings up 274,000,000 results in Google. That's over two hundred million hits. Much as I love what I do, and these words describe my career accurately, they have no place in my X factor statement because they say nothing about what is so special or different about me.

This is no doubt a perfectly sensible way to describe yourself, and please keep using whatever title or descriptor you generally use, except in relation to your X factor.

Your X factor expresses a distinctive combination of qualifications and qualities that is specific to you and could only be you. This means avoiding generic, overused descriptors, which is why I collated my own list of '*100+ Banned X factor words*' that risk diminishing your X factor unless qualified by other descriptors that convey a more restricted, nuanced meaning. (You'll find this list at the back of this book.)

For example, Dale R. Roberts describes himself as 'an indie author, video content creator and self-publishing advocate'. My *100+ Banned X factor words* list includes author, creator and advocate, and 'I am an author, content creator and advocate' would be too generic, but Roberts adds rich detail, so it works. You can include terms in your X factor that apply to many other people, but it is your exclusive combination that makes it yours.

I am fierce about this. Why?

Details matter

A cartoon by Bill Mauldin shows two hoboes. One of them says, 'I started as a simple bum but now I'm hard-core unemployed'. Treat generic business jargon, such as expert, thought leader or analyst, as toxic in your exploration. This applies equally to words professionals use to describe themselves on LinkedIn (speaker, author, coach) and words that are so overused as to be drained of meaning (radical, out of the box, challenger, connector, big-picture thinker). Gather them up in a pile and set on fire.

Time to shouty-cap the point. USING ANY BANNED WORDS WILL DILUTE YOUR X factor OR TURN IT INTO EVERYONE ELSE'S NON-FACTOR. I'm going to own the shouting, as this is important. I'm here to set you up for success and will do whatever it takes to achieve that.

You can, of course, use these terms to describe what you do in the rest of your professional life. I certainly do. But they shouldn't feature as part of your X factor statement, except when qualified by other descriptors that add nuance to provide a more explicit meaning. Miles Rote describes himself in his Facebook profile as a 'wellness gangster, digital nomad and yogi'. The nuances, the contrast of gangster and yogi, the way Rote combines these words, lifts this X factor statement above just another 'wellness influencer, social media expert and yoga teacher' clone.

Conjuring up original word pictures that don't rely on the 100+ Banned X factor words list, like bio-hacker, eco-activist or food waste warrior, can be a huge bonus. These unusual expressions can end up featuring in your final X factor statement. You have already done the work in finding rare idioms that describe what you do. Happy dance.

3X SUPER STEP 1: GATHER

In this first 3X Super Step you gather data by exploring your history and heritage, your hobbies and your (h)interesting facts. You go personal, you go deep and you do these exercises privately.

Remember to be mindful of the trigger warnings noted in the previous chapter and take care of yourself.

3X Super Step 1: Gather — history/heritage

Here you will complete an exercise template that explores your personal history and heritage. This doesn't have to be exotic. From growing up with a single mother in public housing to becoming prime minister. This is the journey of Australian Prime Minister Anthony Albanese. Maybe you come from a family of nine or growing up you went to the beach every Sunday, or you belong to three generations of die-hard Liverpool football supporters. Yes, this is all part of finding your X factor.

Completing the history/heritage exercise should take you about 15 minutes. Devote more time to it if you need to. Points to consider before you start the exercise:

1. Nail nuance.
2. Consider how to stay safe.
3. Explore the art of shape shifting.

Nail nuance

Shantaram is a 2003 autobiographical novel by Gregory David Roberts, in which a convicted Australian bank robber and heroin addict escapes from Pentridge Prison, Australia, and flees to Mumbai (then Bombay), India. For some time the author was a speaker on the business circuit, and through the courtesy of a client I heard him present. Afterwards my client introduced me to him. I shook his hand and told him how much I enjoyed his talk and his book. (I didn't tell him I was from Mumbai.)

He immediately laughed and with a twinkle in his eyes he said, 'I would never mistake you for anything but a South Bombay convent-educated girl'. In one sentence he demonstrated the depth of his understanding of India. Whoa, I've never had such a nuanced nailing of my history and heritage! That's what you are looking for in these exercises. Depth, richness, nuance.

Stay safe

Keep the focus of the questions on positive experiences and memories to stay safe and avoid triggers of unhappiness or even trauma. And answer only the questions you want to or can.

You need to channel 'Queen of Clean' Marie Kondo's vibe from the Netflix original series *Tidying Up with Marie Kondo*. She advocates keeping only what 'sparks joy'. I doubt I'm the only person who rewinds repeatedly to the bit where she shows what sparking joy looks like. 'Ting', she says, her whole body quivering. This sparked a range of funny and dark 'spark joy' memes. While Kondo focuses on organising, let's extend her 'spark joy' palette out into this work too. **What experiences, memories or stories spark joy?**

Shape shift

A few years ago, I was invited to speak at a dairy farmers' event in New Zealand. On the day I enter a room full of burly, ruddy-faced farmers, with lots of flannel shirts and giant work boots. The only young brown woman in the room, I am wearing a pencil-slim dress and heels, hair in a sleek bob (what can I say, my look then). Every time I shook hands, it was like a hand the size of a large steak swallowed mine up to the wrist! When I stepped on stage, I could sense the incredulity in the audience. Exotic inner-city slicker meets true-blue people of the land. What could we ever have in common? But I had redone the history/heritage exercise before I went in. Phew.

My paternal grandfather was a farmer from a small village in Tamil Nadu. Some of my family continue to own and tend the land there. My family (spread all over the globe) has strong connections with the Tamilian idea of *oor*, or a specific place, in this case our ancestral village.

So I started with my grandfather's story and some of the wisdom he passed on to me that came straight from the land. Suddenly the audience saw me for what I am, a farmer's granddaughter, and I shape shifted into one of them. This is the power of your X factor in service of an audience, and how you can tailor your X factor to suit an audience. But it wouldn't have been possible without the rich value of the history/heritage exercise, that you will complete shortly. And you can keep revisiting it and adding layers. Put as much as you can into these exercises, because out of quantity you can extract quality.

When doing this exercise, be specific and detailed. You want rich, juicy details and depth here.

1. Where were you born?
2. Describe your parents'/grandparents' heritage and occupations.
3. What jobs have you had growing up or before your current career?
4. Is there something you or your family are known for (a signature move, a sports team you love, a holiday destination you always went to)?
5. Think of some positive lived experiences you have had. Can you write them up in a few words?
6. Anything else you want to add to this list?

Figure 5.1 History/heritage exercise

Here are some examples to provide more details for questions 4, 5 and 6:

- **Signature move:** Maybe your family is known for doing The Macarena backwards, or for the mullet you all sported in the 1980s.
- **Positive lived experiences:** You might have other happy memories and stories from school, your neighbourhood or your community. This question gives you the space to capture those.
- **Anything else:** The last question in the exercise is your opportunity to dig deep and add in any other information about your history or heritage.

Complete this history/heritage exercise before moving on to the next. Finish each exercise in sequence — it's easier that way.

3X Super Step 1: Gather — hobbies

This exercise invites you to explore your talents, passions and skills. What lights you up? Rock music? True crime podcasts? Knitting?

Here you will:

1. Explore sukha.
2. Look at unusual hobbies.
3. Play with sparking light.
4. Make an inventory of your hobbies and interests.

Completing the hobbies inventory exercise should take you roughly 15 minutes.

Sukha

Associate Professor Mark Lauchs, a criminologist at the Queensland University of Technology, has a research focus on Outlaw Motorcycle Gangs. That's interesting and unusual enough to work in this exercise. Your talent and your work might be instructional design, and you love it (bless you) but this won't draw your audience in. So you can't really use this as part of your X factor statement. Please don't have an existential crisis now; it's just the way of the world.

For your hobbies, don't claim a talent such as being a *writer*, as this has a brag quality. It's also on my *100+ Banned X factor words* list along with *author, content producer, blogger* and variations thereof. Words like this can make you appear as the hero of your own story. You become unrelatable to your audience. It turns them off. They're thinking, *so what*. Sorry, but this fails the who cares test. But don't despair. Writer is sexy. Feel free to use writer in your dating profile but not in your X factor statement.

Time to list all your hobbies and interests. *Sukha*, a Sanskrit word meaning comfortable and relaxed, will be your friend and guide here. Go to your happy place and think about what makes your chest feel buoyant? For me it's Bollywood dancing, Iyengar yoga, exploring nature, regional home-cooked food, reading and the visual arts, to name a few.

Explore your hobbies in your X factor quest because what makes your X factor shiny and authentic is being wholehearted about it. You don't want to include anything you feel 'meh' about.

News raiding

Maybe you have an unusual hobby. They probably don't come much more obscure than 'news raiding', which involves chasing opportunities to appear as a casual bystander in the background of television news reports. In this very niche area, Paul Yarrow, a South Londoner, is a world record holder. Yarrow has often featured in the background of various live news events. News raiding is like the live version of photo bombing. It's uncommon because it's hard to pull off the combination of ear to the ground, gall and sheer good luck needed to pursue this hobby.

Other examples of unusual, niche hobbies are beetle fighting, extreme ironing, stone skipping (yes, just as it says), competitive duck herding, or element collecting (from the periodic table; I know, WTF!). Remember, this will likely be fresh and interesting for your audience. Audiences love stuff they can amuse their friends with at their next dinner party. Hobby outliers are a great source of this social capital.

So how do you turn your audiences on, rather than off? By making sure whatever you use supports your message and helps your audience connect with you and remember what you're saying. I'll explore this further in later chapters. Exactly how you demo live duck herding in a conference room is a challenge I leave with you. It's like the conundrum that Nicolas Cage faces in the movie *Adaptation*, where his twin (also played by Cage) has an idea for a script that sounds fine on paper but is impossible to pull off in either real or reel life.

Sparking a light

Another avenue to explore is past hobbies. You might have been mad about the guitar and learned it as a teenager but have done nothing with it since. This can be added to your 'Maybe' list. Don't write it off yet. Who knows, it might work.

Here's a beautiful quote by 'purposologist' Alexander den Heijer: 'You often feel tired, not because you've done too much, but because you've done too little of what sparks a light in you.' This is the lens to use when looking at your hobbies. Choose what sparks a light in you.

> **Make an inventory of your hobbies and interests, being as specific as possible.**
> 1. What do you do for leisure? Make a list.
> 2. What musical instruments can you play?
> 3. What talents do you have?
> 4. What performances have you given?
> 5. What sports or sport teams do you follow?
> 6. What were your hobbies as a kid?
> 7. What would you love to learn as a hobby?
> 8. What hobbies have you tried unsuccessfully to learn?

Figure 5.2 Hobbies Inventory exercise

Make sure you complete the hobbies inventory exercise before moving to the next exercise. It is best to do the exercises one by one, spending time on each. Also, you can get overwhelmed trying to do all the exercises together at the end.

3X Super Step 1: Gather — (h)interesting facts

Hard Quiz is one of Australia's favourite game shows. Each episode features four contestants, each with a specialist subject area. Part of the success of the show is host Tom Gleeson's acerbic wit and the contestants' often countercultural, obscure, nerdy subjects. Vintage washing machines, anyone?

Here you will:

1. Explore the fine art of nerding out.
2. Discover why cafés are boring.
3. Complete an exercise to capture your nerd interests.

The exercise for this step should take you about 15 minutes.

Nerding out

If you were a *Hard Quiz* contestant, what would your expert subject be? Mid-twentieth-century furniture? The *Toy Story* films? Streaky bacon? This is the time to dive deep into something unusual, nerdy or quirky about you. It doesn't have to be big. This is where a lot of my clients hit their X factor gold. So work on this. Don't rush it. You'll be surprised how much comes to mind. When one of my client's nerds out on eight-hour slow-cooked beef rendang, they can enthuse for hours without drawing breath. It sets their soul on fire!

Cafés are boring

Specificity is the key to this exercise. I cannot stress this enough. A friend signed up for a few dating apps when looking to meet someone in Melbourne and noticed how many people had as their interest 'cafés'. Yup, just that. I know Melbourne has a fabulous café culture and everyone has their favourite local but listing cafés collectively as your hobby reeks of boring.

Compare this with someone who offers 'New Orleans Style Cold-Brew Coffee Connoisseur but will drink hot lattes for love'. That detail tells us volumes about the person. They are committed to coffee, and in the struggle between thriftiness and coffee snobbery, snobbery wins, as cold brew is almost three times the price of normal coffee. They can plan (cold brew can take up to 24 hours to make, but it's also less fiddly, set and forget). They could have sensitive digestion, as cold coffee is smooth, with low levels of acidity. (I know, too much information!) All this from that one insight into their hobby. What balances this extreme dedication is their willingness, at least on paper, to tolerate regular coffee for the sake of love. Aww!

Time to capture some of your nerd interests through an exercise.

(H)interesting facts means going nerdy and detailed. Compare the more generic term cyclist with a specialist vibe of cycle path nerd.

1. What topics can you nerd out on?
2. What are some of your quirks? (Can't sit with your back to the door?)
3. What is one unusual thing about you?
4. What is your party trick?
5. What is your party trick after imbibing alcohol?

Figure 5.3   (H)interesting facts exercise

This exercise should take you at least 15 minutes to complete.

3X Super Step 1: Gather — checkpoint

Let's look at the data you have gathered so far.

3X Super Step 1: Gather	What you should have	*Time allocation (estimate)
History/heritage	Completed history/heritage exercise	15 minutes
Hobbies	Completed hobbies inventory exercise	15 minutes
(H)interesting facts	Completed (h)interesting facts exercise	15 minutes

Figure 5.4 Gather checkpoint

The more time you allocate to each exercise, the richer and deeper your answers will be. Of course. But what that means is so will your X factor statement.

FALLOW TIME

In a classic clip from an old *I Love Lucy* show, Lucy gets a job in a chocolate factory, and they place her and her friend Ethel on the assembly line. The draconian supervisor tells them, 'Girls, this is your last chance. If one piece of candy gets past you unwrapped, you're fired!' The production line starts and they carefully wrap candy, remarking how easy it is. Then the assembly line speeds up, and they can no longer keep up. They stuff their mouths with candy and Lucy calls out to her friend in despair, 'Ethel, I think we're fighting a losing game'. They hide the candy under their hats and even down the front of their dresses. Their mouths are bulging when the supervisor returns. Seeing the empty conveyor belt, in a moment of perfectly timed comedy, the supervisor shouts to the conveyor belt operator, 'Speed it up!'

What makes this sketch funny even now is the relevance of its message to modern life. You too may want to go faster and faster and cram everything in, especially when the end is in sight.

At this point I'm going to invite you to take a step back from the work. Zoom right out and look at what you have collected from the history/heritage, hobbies and (h) interesting facts exercises. Spread it all out in front of you.

Australian Indigenous artists often use a bird's-eye perspective. That's what you need to do now. Here's a bird's eye view of my list. Note this is an edited version of my shortlist. My long list is several pages long.

Heritage	I'm Indian. That's true of 1.5 billion people. I'm also Australian-Indian (that's 700,000 people).
Hobbies	I'm a Bollywood-dancing Indian.
(H)interesting facts	I'm an economist by training and for the past 15 years have worked as a business storyteller.

Figure 5.5 Bird's eye view

Once you have stepped back from your work and gained a bird's-eye view of it, I'm going to ask you to do the most dangerous thing an author can do. Stop reading. Take a break before you proceed. Why? 'Fallow time is necessary to grow everything from actual crops to figurative ones, like writing, like any work,' said writer Bonnie Tsui in a recent *New York Times* article.

Fallow time invites you to take time out from what you're doing. This allows your unconscious to do some of the heavy lifting. If possible, leave all the completed exercises in plain sight. Read them once over before taking a break. Then continue to the next 3X Super Step to make your data zing.

3X SUPER STEP 2: ZING

In this 3X Super Step you will:

- highlight zing words
- create single circles and interlink circles
- build shortlist word combinations.

1. Highlight zing words

History/Heritage	Hobbies	(H)interesting facts
———☐	———☐	———☐
———☐	———☐	———☐
———☐	———☐	———☐
———☐	———☐	———☐

2. Create single circles and interlink circles

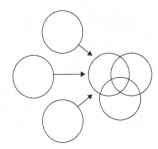

3. Build shortlist word combinations

Figure 5.6 3X Super Step 2: Zing

3X Super Step 2: Zing — highlight zing words

Spread out the completed exercises from 3X Super Step 1. This is your field research and includes data from your history/heritage, hobbies and (h)interesting facts exercises.

Review the exercises and highlight keywords. Words with a buzz, words that excite you, words that are interesting. These are your zing words. Zing words are bursting with potential. Bollywood dancer, eco explorer, cloud obsessed — If you metaphorically touched a zing word it would fizz like champagne. Comedians will land a joke on a zing — the funniest words, guaranteeing a laugh. To borrow from jazz composer Duke Ellington's hit from the 1930s, 'It don't mean a thing if it ain't got that ZING'.

Keep in mind that the bar is low in the professional world. Your zing words don't have to be dramatic or over the top. Be light and free. Don't overthink it. Shortly I will share Sandy McDonald's example.

With highlighted zing words in hand, move to the exercise below, in which you will place these zing words into circles. This will allow you to play with and form different combinations with your zing words.

3X Super Step 2: Zing — create single circles and interlink circles

Follow these steps to create your single circles:

1. Place each zing word in its own circle.
2. Use the template provided online or at the end of this book.
3. Use one word or phrase per circle.
4. Put as many words or phrases into circles as possible.

5. Go for quantity.
6. Review your zing words. Can any others be highlighted and added in circles?

Look closely at your completed single circle list. Time to punch up the words, by deleting any jargon —writer, radical thinker. Once you've created your single-circle list, the next step is to interlink these circles. You interlink the circles to explore possible relationships between what you have so far. Experiment by interlinking as many combinations as possible.

Follow these steps to interlink three circles:

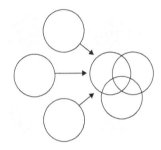

1. Interlink three-word circles at a time.
2. Don't group words, go random.
3. Use the template provided online or at the end of this book.
4. Interlink as many three-word circles as you can; go crazy.
5. Work quickly.
6. Experiment. Go for quantity and think laterally.
7. Don't edit.
8. This is your long list, for your eyes only.

Revisit your zing words, your single-circle list and your interlinking circles. Is there anything you can add, edit or remove?

Give your completed single circles list (not the interlinking circles) to your partner or a trusted friend (teenage children are great at this). Ask them to form as many interlinking circles of these as possible. Be prepared: they will be looser and freer, as it's not their list.

Compare your interlinked circles with those they have made. Highlight the interlinking circles that stand out for you. What is memorable, distinctive, fresh? Go back to the exercises you completed in the previous chapter. Did you miss anything that could be added? Now move to the next exercise, in which you will shortlist your best word combinations from your interlinking circles.

3X Super Step 2: Zing — shortlist word combinations

An X factor, as I have shown, can take many forms. But for our purposes here I am going to ask you to pick a few words or phrases from the exercises above, a shortlist of your best word or phrase combinations.

In the next chapter I will guide you towards crafting your X factor into a statement that embodies three ideas that represent you, combining to create a portrait or representation that is distinctive and individual to you. To do that you need to have a shortlist of word/phrase combinations to work with:

1. From the interlinking circles, create a shortlist of your favourite word or phrase combinations. Choose about a dozen. You can always come back and choose new words as you go.
2. Combine different words and phrases. Do they work when spoken aloud? Play with hashtags.
3. Is it specific enough? Is it true?

4. Alliterations work a treat ('Zumba-dancing, Zimbabwean-born, zebra-loving zealot').
5. Write these combinations next to your name in a pretend CV.
6. Run your top three options past a trusted mentor, colleague or family member.

Sandy McDonald provides story clarity coaching and training to build communication skills through purposeful, contextualised storytelling. She calls herself 'The Story Whisperer'.

Her handwritten workings below illustrate how her X factor started to emerge and take shape.

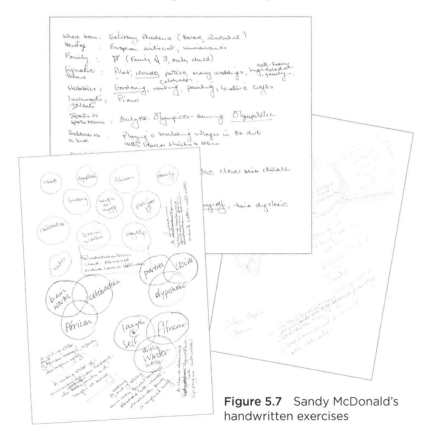

Figure 5.7 Sandy McDonald's handwritten exercises

This is the one time when working towards crafting a statement with a combination of the words or phrases will serve you best. My experience with clients has proven time and time again that once you have an X factor statement, you can then find myriad ways of using that statement in your presentation and across your professional and personal life. I don't claim this is the only way to discover your X factor, but my clients tell me it is the simplest and best way to guarantee results.

The first step to crafting an X factor statement is choosing a few words and phrases from the exercises above. At this stage it may be hard for you to commit to a couple of phrases, but you need to narrow down your options. It's time to make some choices. Remember, nothing is permanent. You can always revisit your list later.

Your X factor is taking shape, feeling more solid and individual to you. Working through the exercises in this chapter and the next is how Sandy arrived at 'Zimbabwean-born, cloud-obsessed orchid cacti cultivator'. This is her reflection on the process.

CASE STUDY

THE STORY WHISPERER

Sandy McDonald, the story whisperer, shares her experience of unearthing her X factor using Yamini's 3X Super Steps process

'What do you think your X factor is?' Yamini asked us. It seemed like an innocuous enough question, but within seconds my brain hit nutri-bullet mode. A sludge of thoughts — remnants of past desires, slivers of unfulfilled potential, half-eaten, not-yet-celebrated talents. An indigestible mix of if onlys and still-to-bes.

As if Yamini was reading the turmoil, she asked us to follow a process and jot down on a piece of paper all the ideas we had about what made us. We weren't to order or strategise the words or thoughts or memories, just put them down as they came into our minds.

Out of the sludge emerged a slew of seemingly unrelated words. Family, clouds, celebration, dirt, colour ...

How, I wondered, would any of this help me determine my X factor?

I have been speaking for ten years. Feedback suggests my content hits the mark, but what about me? Do I leave an impression after I leave the stage? Do my audience think about who I am and want to know more? Do they instantly request to connect with me on LinkedIn, join my Facebook page, buy my book?

I'd always thought the response I got, although modest, was enough. But perhaps not. Not if I could access my X factor.

When someone like Brené Brown hits the stage, she leaves a blank space when she leaves. You want her to stay, to know more about her. You wonder what it would be like to be her friend. Clearly she has an X factor.

We went on to put our words together into groups of three. Very quickly the three ideas that sang out were my African heritage, clouds and gardening. Didn't sound remotely X factorish to me.

Then Yamini began to work her magic. She looked at the words. Clearly they were more than words to her, they were descriptors of something much bigger. She asked insightful questions, dug down and juxtaposed the ideas, and extracted:

- Zimbabwean
- cloud-obsessed
- orchid cacti cultivator.

What is so extraordinary about this X factor description is that on its own, yes, it completely encapsulates so much about what is individual, different about me. But it is more than that.

Zimbabwean talks to a beloved heritage and a troubled disconnection. I'm white with a missionary heritage. In today's world, that doesn't exactly equate to a badge of honour. Still, I share the stories that illuminate this experience. For my audiences, I speak to lives that are not binary, but multi-layered and complicated. My stories seek to raise awareness of the plight of those I left behind.

My father was a pilot. For most of my life I plied the skies above Africa sitting behind him. The cloud sets were extraordinary, staggering formations, and wonderful colours. He navigated the clouds alert for dangers, I for design and artistry. Today I still scan the skies, inspired by the nuances of the weather's stories.

Dirt, digging and mud were my delight in childhood. Now, I make soil and cultivate every cutting I can find. From a few small leaves, we have an exotic garden of orchid cacti.

There is something powerful about creating so much abundance from so little. That speaks to how I want to live my life, in our era of waste and destruction, for growth, restoration and regeneration.

Through this simple process, Yamini led me to my X factor and all that will inform my stories going forward. It fills me with delight and changes what is possible for me, my presentations and my work.

Take your left hand over your chest and pat yourself on your back. Well done.

You have put in the hard yards and have completed the two foundational steps in our 3X Super Steps process. You will cover 3X Super Step 3: Craft in detail in the next chapter.

I. Gather	✅
II. Zing	✅
III. Craft	Next chapter

Figure 5.8 3X Super Steps — chapter checkpoint

You have gathered your data and made it zing. Having completed the exercises in this chapter you now have a word combination shortlist. In the next chapter I will guide you towards crafting your X factor into an eloquent statement using some of these shortlisted words.

CHAPTER 6

CRAFT YOUR X FACTOR STATEMENT

The shampoo ad says, 'It won't happen overnight, but it will happen'. You may stamp your feet impatiently as you watch the model flick a gorgeous mane of lush locks over her face... or is it just me? The truth is, finding your X factor usually takes time.

Because I did not have this book to guide me, my X factor took 15 years to emerge. That need not be your fate. There's another clear path forward. This chapter shares my secrets so you can speed up the discovery process. You can accelerate forward and I'll show you how to do this safely, in small steps, through many tiny iterations.

Welcome to Lab You. The scientist for these experiments is you, and initially the safe space of your home is your lab. Here you will craft and recraft the word and phrase combinations you shortlisted in the previous chapter into your X factor statement.

Entering Lab You is like cracking the spine of a new book, setting off on a journey full of adventure and promise. Travel light and pack only an experimental mindset.

EXPERIMENTAL MINDSET

In an old Indian parable six blind men try to figure out what an elephant must look like. Surrounding the unfamiliar animal, each of them reaches out and touches a different part of its body and describes the elephant based on this direct but limited evidence. For the first blind man, who falls against its side, the elephant is like a wall; the second, who grasps a tusk, compares it to a spear; the third, who finds its writhing trunk, is reminded of a snake; the fourth touches a knee and is convinced the animal is like a tree; the fifth man, who happens to run his hand over an ear, believes it is like a fan; the sixth seizes its tail and insists the animal is more like a rope.

They are all right, yet all quite wrong. Your individual experience of your X factor and what you end up with is going to differ from anyone else's. You must be open to all possibilities. Anything is possible if, and only if, you are open to it.

A light hand

Lab You is about one thing and one thing only: experimentation. **What serves you best here is a light hand and a sense of fun and play, mischief even.** Do the exercises, but don't hustle for your X factor statement. You cannot wrestle it to the ground, as it will recede every time you get too earnest or serious. This is its nature. Your work coaxes it to emerge from the shadows, to shape shift from a hologram to a solid, three-dimensional form.

The main trail

There are of course practical applications for your X factor in your day-to-day work, your presentations and your business. And these matter, as they deliver business results. But as you wade far into the weeds in your experimentation, don't lose sight of the main trail. Finding your X factor is transformational. This was bestselling book coach Kath Walters' experience. Once she had unearthed her X factor 'bike path nerd, still water kayaker and power napper', she began using *bike path nerd* as a metaphor in her work to grab people's attention and to lighten up complex ideas. All instant business applications. But it also shifted her view of herself and what is possible. She now says, 'My dream is to have a six-lane bike path freeway'. No one could have predicted that Kath would have crystallised this vision at the start of the process. **You can soar with your X factor; it gives you wings if you let it.**

It can change how you see yourself as a presenter. Your identity. Nothing drives behaviour more than identity, who you see yourself as, and who you want the world to see you as. Everything you say is filtered through this new lens, which takes you in new directions. It can permeate everything you do and change you forever.

This kind of X factor gives your audience a gilded stairway from your professional to your personal persona. **When you start your X factor quest, you cannot imagine the doors it will open for you.** In the immortal words of Ygritte, in *Game of Thrones*, 'You know nothing, John Snow'!

Intersectionality

Crafting your X factor statement needs an experimental approach because it lives in intersectionality (where different parts of your identity meet). As you play with the ideas below, I invite you to stay true to who you are. Too much people pleasing, diluting your X factor in the hope of gaining everyone's approval, will land you in vanilla land.

Hard message. **Not everyone is going to love you, and that's okay, but more people will love you with than without X factor.** If you try to please everyone, you end up aiming for the LCD (lowest common denominator). LCD is the opposite of X factor; it is everything X factor is not, and everything you do not want. You can 'smart down' your X factor (and I'll show you how), but don't water it down.

SHARPEN AND DEEPEN

Every X factor statement contains three elements: individual words or phrases. Look at this breakdown of my statement.

X factor statement
World's only **economist** turned **Bollywood-dancing** business storyteller
Elements (word or phrase combinations) of the statement
1. Economist
2. Bollywood dancing
3. Business storyteller

Figure 6.1 My X factor statement and its elements

Just as a jeweller polishes a diamond before setting it, you must polish your shortlist of word combinations, the potential elements of your X factor statement before you can set them into a statement.

So there's still work to do before you can craft your first X factor statement. This work sharpens your word/phrase combinations. You do this through:

- palette play
- specificity sparkles
- contrast.

Let's look at these tips individually and then, through a case study, see how it all comes together.

Palette play

In your word shortlist, play with the palette of words. Search for synonyms and try different combinations. Quantity gives you quality. Punch up and sharpen expression, but don't give in to the temptation to make up words. Any fans of the long-running 1990s sitcom *Friends*? In season 4, cast members challenge Monica and Rachel on what Chandler's job really is. The two shriek in horror at the question, and after a few vague, desperate guesses, Rachel calls him a 'transponster'. Along with the rest of us, no one on *Friends* knew what Chandler did for a living, for nine seasons. But you can be sure he wasn't a transponster ('That's not even a wooord!'). Don't make up words; your audience will lose their minds and you will lose your credibility.

What about portmanteaus, words that join and combine the meaning of two other words? Kris Jenner, the brains behind the Kardashian franchise, describes herself as a 'momanger': a mom + manager. Portmanteaus in an X factor statement feel contrived and may have your audience scratching their head in confusion. The only portmanteau I recommend is brunch.

You can be imaginative, though. If you were on *Top Gun*, what would your call sign be? Rooster? Maverick? Eagle? Mine is Tiger. When I was five years old, I travelled daily to school on a big red bus. I always imagined the bus was a tiger, which inspired my call sign.

If you were a spy, what would your code name be? Mine is Quantum. No, you can't have it. I got there first. Also, if more than one spy is called Quantum, that will confuse, no? You may never use this as part of your X factor, but do let these ideas explode your palette on what is possible.

Specificity sparkles

'A dog ate my lunch', my client Jen once tweeted. She soon replaced it with 'A Dalmatian ate my burrito' …and Twitter exploded. People loved it. Why?

What separated those two tweets and transformed *ho hum* into *ha*? The magic happened when she became *specific*. Being specific creates an emotional response. It makes people *feel* something. Specificity paints a picture, which helps people to see clearly what you're saying.

Being specific is the key to X factor success. It sounds easy, but it's a stumbling block for many professionals. You're often good with the big picture, the abstract and the general. But for your X factor elements to be strong, resonant and true to you it must be small picture, concrete and specific. Your audience should be able to see it and feel it, to 'walk in its shoes'. Think of the X factor elements in various statements I have shared so far: Still water kayaker, river swimmer, cloud obsessed. Each of these paints a picture, they are sensory and specific. You can 'see' them in your mind's eye.

With each of the words on your shortlist drill down, down, down until you are so specific that the image created could *only* be you, no one else, not even your twin if you have one.

Maybe you worry about getting too specific. *Will this still be relatable for my audience? Shouldn't stuff be universal so everyone can relate?* Whether it's a script for a Hollywood movie or your X factor statement, you must package the universal in the specific so your audience can connect with it. Specific makes it relatable for your audience. Being specific unlocks magic. **An X factor statement without specific sensory elements is like a diamond without sparkle.**

Contrast

Check for word combinations that provide contrast. Imagine an opera-trained singer and death metal fan. The image of those two worlds colliding sets off fireworks in your audience's heads. It piques their curiosity. How does an opera buff also live in the death metal world? Using contrast raises your X factor a level. It provides a twist, as the contrast is surprising.

Artists achieve contrast by juxtaposing contrasting elements. Dan Scott, founder of Draw Paint Academy, explains, 'Contrast is everything in art. Without it, you may as well leave the canvas blank'. An artist might place the colours red and green next to each other as the contrasting colours make the image pop. Contrast focuses your audience's attention and creates drama and excitement. Contrast can tell a story and create individuality.

By surprising your audience, contrast create tension in your X factor. So much content washes over us because of its sheer predictability. Surprise is a secret weapon against information saturation. How often does a presentation surprise or delight you, as an audience member? The answer is probably rarely. A simple yet potent way to harness the power of surprise is through contrast.

Using contrast in your statement is like throwing a hand grenade into the mix: it makes your X factor explode.

Let's look at a case study that pulls all this together.

CASE STUDY

MARIAM ISSA

Mariam Issa is a speaker, author, storyteller and community builder. Mariam worked through the X factor process with me and we had a lot of fun.

One of her bios includes this summary:

> From Somalia's war-torn Mogadishu to the world's most liveable city, Melbourne, to strengthening my cultural currency through sharing the wealth of my nation (CookwithMariam), to opening my backyard as a community garden and providing a healing space for women, to authoring *A Resilient Life*, to founding Mariam Issa, a brand of storytelling to unlock potential, I passionately believe all we need to overcome adversity is to stretch our imagination.

As I worked through the process with Mariam, X factor statement options emerged along the way. I'm sharing these with you to illustrate some of the behind-the-scenes work that can help you polish what you have. Each iteration gets stronger.

Version 1: Horn of Africa born global nomad, numerologist
Love the specificity of Horn of Africa. Global nomad indicates she has lived in multiple places and cultures around the world. But as a descriptor it feels too general. Numerologist is an interesting, unexpected element.

Version 2: Descended from nomadic African camel herders, now rooted in a Brighton community garden
What works here is the specific detail of camel herders, the contrast between nomadic and rooted and between African and Melbourne. Starting in Africa and finishing in a Melbourne Garden provides perfect book ends.

But wait, there's more. Mariam told me her mother would often say, 'If you host someone in your heart, you can host them in your house'. By that she meant that people will wrong you, but you need to forgive and not cut the ties. Learn to do this with boundaries: not everyone can be 'hosted in your heart'. We experimented with this idea in the next iteration.

Version 3: Hosting people in her heart and building community in her open garden in Melbourne's Bayside
This iteration is anchored by the specificity of place, contrasting garden with heart, the physical and the emotional, the idea of being a heart host (heart hosting is not physical hosting), married with the act of physical hosting in nature.

When I ran these versions by a small focus group, they found version 3 the least relatable, as they didn't understand what 'hosting in her heart' meant. Mariam and I had made the classic mistake of overcooking her X factor.

The winner was version 2. Besides ticking all our boxes, it does the most important thing an X factor should do: it opens doors, invites questions and provokes conversations.

Once you have sharpened your words you are ready for the final step in the 3X Super Step process. I'm now going to ask you to do one of the most important things in this book. It marks the difference between action heroes and wannabes on our quest.

3X SUPER STEP 3: CRAFT

Spread out all the work you have done so far before you, then walk away from it. Make yourself a cup of tea, walk the dog, call a friend. Don't be like a pit bull on a pant leg. Let go for a while. Take a break and wander off ... but do please come back. Thank you.

When you return, look at the sea of gold before you. Take a deep breath and write up the first draft of your X factor statement. This should have:

- a combination of three words or phrases
- one or two specific, sensory words that paint a picture
- at least one contrast between elements.

I understand that X factor is a shape shifter and can take many forms, and there is no magic one size fits all. But at this point what is most useful, what will help you move forward, is to craft your X factor as a statement that combines three ideas to create a portrait or representation of you. Take a leaf out of the playbook of tech firms that create a minimum viable product to test a market. At this stage all you need is a minimum viable X factor statement. Think of this as your personal tag line. None of your choices need be final. You have a vault of gold that you can always dip into and select other options.

This part of the process is an art, not a science. The principles I provide below 'are more what you'd call guidelines than actual rules', to quote Captain Barbossa from *Pirates of the Caribbean*.

This is your first go. Be kind to yourself. No one else need see it. Now, working quickly, keep experimenting with the statement. Aim to create 25, 50, even 75 variations. Try changing the word order, replacing a word with a sharper synonym, checking for contrast and sensory detail. Create 15 variations simply by changing your first word and another 15 variations by changing your last word.

When you've finished, select your top three X factor statements. Write them down on sticky notes and put them up strategically around the house, on your desk, the fridge, the bathroom mirror. Keep the notes in your line of sight for a few days and note what works and what doesn't, what jumps out at you and what other ideas float up. Live with your statements for a few days as you continue to craft and recraft them using the techniques following.

Modern art and boy bands

Have you ever looked at a piece of modern art, scratched your head and persuaded yourself that you, or even your five-year-old, could have done that? Your response is a win for the artist. The art is successful because you, the viewer, relate to it. It calls to you and challenges you. A bestselling kitchen towel bears the legend 'Modern art, you could have done it, but you didn't'. You probably couldn't really do it. What matters is you think you could.

You want that same quality in your X factor statement. An ideal statement needs to be **relatable**, **aspirational** and **inspirational**. How is that possible? How can you pack so much into so little? Your best bet is to learn from, I'm going to say this slowly, boy bands. Yes, boy bands. Think Backstreet Boys, One Direction, BTS. Amongst all the boy band eye candy there is one member who looks extra cute, one who can dance and, oh, one who can sing (or can he?).

Just like boy band members, while all the words/phrases in your X factor statement are stars, each performs a different role. For an ideal X factor statement, aim for one word that is relatable, one word that is aspirational and one word that is inspirational. This is best practice. Don't panic if you're not there yet.

As motivational speaker Norman Vincent Peale said, 'Shoot for the moon. Even if you miss, you'll land among the stars.'

Table 6.2 illustrates the quality each of these words brings to your statement.

Note that you're not setting out to manipulate your audience or force fit words to this formula. These are guidelines only.

Word	Quality	Works to	Audience reaction
Relatable	Warm	Opens doors	Ahh 😈
Aspirational	Wacky	Sparks desire	Oh 🙂
Inspirational	Wow	Inspires dreams	Wow 🤩

Table 6.2 Boy band X factor statement words

An X factor statement works when it opens doors to your audience's hearts, desires and dreams. It makes them feel connected to it and to you. Chris Huet is a speaker, a fighter pilot and a poet. That's exciting, but he makes it relatable and aspirational to his audiences by saying, 'I help people speak with the precision of a fighter pilot and the passion of a poet'. In this context the unadorned word *speaker* works because Chris is also a fighter pilot and a poet. As I said, there is an art to crafting an X factor statement.

The last column indicates how your audience feels when they read or experience an X factor statement containing words that are relatable, aspirational and inspirational. Come on, say it with me. Open your mouth and go 'Ahh', 'Oh', 'Wow'.

Relatable

Check if one of your words or phrases is 'warm' and relatable, makes your audience go ahh, opens their heart (for example, 'farmer's son'). Please avoid being twee or contrived with this. It must be from the heart.

Relatable words serve to counterbalance other words in your X factor by indicating humility. They can stop a statement feeling like a brag. Sometimes in my work a client will craft an X factor statement that has an element or word that feels like it is status or even virtue signalling. Yet the words are based on the client's truth, and I don't want them to change the element or leave it out. For example, 'descended from three generations of soccer legends'. In this instance I will invite them to consider a 'warm' word to balance this. Warm words make people feel connected to you.

Aspirational and inspirational

To provide contrast one element needs to be aspirational; your audience thinks, *oh, maybe I could do that*. Aspirational words provoke curiosity and questions. 'Urban beekeeper' has people thinking, *hmm, I've always wanted to meet one*. A 'river swimmer'? Many people have happy childhood associations with water and feel nostalgic for a lake or river they splashed about in as kids. *I could swim in my river, but I don't.* It took a Carolyn Tate (ex-banker turned purpose pioneer, river-swimming activist) to make this aspirational. An aspirational element in your statement prompts your audience to think, *I wish I could ... and maybe I can*. They don't river swim, but they could; they have never tried Bollywood dancing, but they could.

For a blockbuster X factor statement one element needs to be inspirational. Your audience goes, *wow, I wish I had thought of that*. Russell Pearson is an Australian-based artist, strategist, designer and masterful presenter. Russell describes himself as a 'business blacksmith'. Inspiring, distinctive, and desirable.

Please don't worry if none of your words have these qualities. You can always come back and work on them further. Don't force fit words or move away from your truth. There's nothing more powerful in an X factor statement than staying true to who you are.

Overdoing it can make your statement feel too slick or contrived. I have seen this over and over with my clients. None of their words fit neatly into any of these categories, but the overall statement has X factor. Sometimes, the whole is bigger than the individual parts. If picking a word that's relatable, a word that's aspirational and an inspirational word works for you, please use it. If it doesn't, I have other tips for you that will help. There are different ways of approaching your statement, and this is just one way.

The audience journey

The order in which you present your X factor statement matters. Is there a hook in your first word or phrase? One way to start is to think of this first word or phrase as the beginning of your story. Carolyn Tate's X factor statement is 'Ex-banker turned purpose pioneer, river-swimming activist'. It's a mini journey that began with her leaving banking.

Choose the word you finish on wisely. This is what your audience will remember, like that last note in a piece of music. 'Activist' is a strong word that evokes hope and the promise of change.

The X factor statement version on this book cover wasn't my first attempt. Working through this process is how I arrived at *Bollywood-dancing storytelling economist*. I then flipped this statement on its head to read '*The world's only economist turned Bollywood-dancing business storyteller*'.

This arrangement takes my audience on my journey from economist to business storyteller.

My starting point gives everyone hope: if an economist can find their X factor, anyone can! It suggests how everyone can have an X factor journey, starting from where they are now. It also gives me the authority to write a book boldly titled *X factor*. And I also wanted to wrap up with what I am now, a business storyteller.

Mona Lisa and al dente pasta

The *Mona Lisa* is possibly the most famous painting in the world. There's something about that mysterious smile and imperfect face. Her complete lack of eyebrows and eyelashes, her yellowing skin and receding hair have invited speculation from medical experts. The work is also unfinished, yet it is undoubtedly a masterpiece, a work of extraordinary beauty that brings joy to the millions who crowd into the largest display room in the Louvre, the Salle des États, just for a glimpse.

Just as the *Mona Lisa* is imperfect, your X factor statement works best if it is slightly raw, rather than overcooked. This keeps it authentic and edgy. Working with clients over time I have learned how important it is not to aim for perfection with your X factor. It shouldn't be too neat. Don't smooth down all the edges. It must feel visceral. If you perfect the statement, it becomes 'sanitised', too much like every other scripted piece of communication or spin.

This may seem counterintuitive, as every fibre of your being will want to polish, polish, polish, but resist the temptation. Your first few bashes at your X factor statement are probably going to be your best versions. The more you work on it, buff it and try to tie it all up with a neat bow, the less powerful it will be. In the Mariam Issa case study, I overcooked her X factor. We then reverted to the slightly rawer but more authentic version. The best X factor statements are like perfectly cooked pasta. Not raw or overcooked, but *al dente*.

Now it's about them

Every word in your X factor statement carries a positive or negative charge. It will either attract an audience or repel them. For example, the word *writer* can come across as a brag and distance you from your audience. Instead of a campfire, drawing people in, it's like a ring of frost keeping them out. All my guidelines are about context, though. Why is 'writer' a brag but not 'economist', you might ask? Anyone can claim to be a writer, there are no or low barriers to entry, whereas an economist needs specific qualifications. In my case *economist* works to balance and provide gravitas for what follows (*Bollywood-dancing, storyteller*).

Writer is on my *100+ Banned X factor words* list, and a Google search brings up 5,000,000,000 results. Five Billion! Add nuance, though, and you can use it. See, I'm not heartless.

Di Percy describes herself on her website as a poet, author and corporate mentor with long experience in psychology, business, leadership education and governance. One of her X factor statements is 'mountain writer, forest dweller, soul worker'. Her nuanced 'mountain writer' is fresh and intriguing. I admit I was initially unsure of it, as its meaning is not immediately obvious. But when Di tested it with her audience they loved it, so it works for her context and she left it in.

If you are unsure, test your statement with your target audience. You might be shocked that I haven't considered audience till this point in the book. So many aspects about finding your X factor run counter to conventional business wisdom.

In business settings you should consider your audience first and early. But for X factor success my work has repeatedly shown that you must go personal first. Why? Starting with your audience in mind can dilute and even destroy your X factor. You will immediately start to wonder how your audience will respond. What if they don't like it? In this instance, starting with your audience will find you playing safe in the shallows, sticking to the shoreline, instead of doing a deep, risky dive for gold.

Go personal, dive for gold then bring that back up to the surface and work with it. First find and refine your X factor statement into its truest form. That's what I have worked on with you through all these chapters. Then you can test it on your audience, as Di did.

Once you have your X factor in its pure form, you can curate it for different audiences. For example, some of my audiences want, love and buy my services as an 'economist turned Bollywood-dancing business storyteller'. They want all these elements in my keynote presentations. Other audiences only want to connect with me as an 'economist turned storyteller'.

Carolyn Tate originally had 'Birrarung River swimming, earthy, eco-feminist', before focusing it down to 'Ex-banker turned river-swimming, eco explorer'. Her latest iteration is 'Ex-banker turned purpose pioneer, river-swimming activist'.

This is the beauty of your X factor statement. It evolves and deepens over time. Don't expect this to happen in one go. Be gentle with yourself and give yourself permission to play with the elements in your statement.

The rule of three

When you reach this part of the process, it can be overwhelming. You have so much good stuff, you want to pack it all into your X factor statement. Soon it morphs from a statement to a paragraph, or even a small book. Cease and desist.

It helps to follow the rule of three for each variation of your X factor statement. According to this rule, ideas presented in threes are more interesting, more enjoyable and more memorable for your audience. See how I just used the rule to make the point. 'Friends, Romans, Countrymen'; 'blood, sweat and tears'; 'Location, location, location' — I'm sure you can think of countless other examples.

Mariam Issa's X factor statement contains three multi-word ideas:

- **Idea 1:** Descended from African nomadic camel herders
- **Idea 2:** now rooted in a Brighton
- **Idea 3:** open garden.

A statement with a single idea can also work if it's strong and exclusive. A poster for Tuscan tenor Andrea Bocelli's tour of Australia says simply, 'the world's most beloved tenor'. One large X factor. Bocelli is also 'the biggest selling classical artist of all time'. These single X factors soar as high as the Empire State Building. Nothing need be added.

But in most cases an X factor statement with only one element will feel too limited, without the heft of Bocelli's example. An X factor statement with two word ideas feels unfinished or unbalanced. More than three ideas in your X factor statement and you lose your audience.

If you end up with a paragraph's worth of gold, write up several X factor statements, each using three idea combinations. Using the rule of three, you will end up with a series of short, sharp and punchy X factor statements.

GETTING UNSTUCK

Sometimes you might feel stuck. You have various word combinations, but you just can't make them work. Nothing feels right. Here's what to do to get unstuck:

- Check that your words are not too businessy. Remove any business words, go back to your field research in the 3X Super Steps and highlight words that are personal. Even one business word can be toxic for your statement at this stage.
- Ensure you include specific and sensory words. A statement will not feel strong if it does not have one or two sensory words. Compare 'nature lover' (that's most people), 'garden enthusiast' (still too generic) versus 'orchid cacti cultivator'. The last is a sensory diamond.
- Use a metaphor. Sometimes you are trying to pin down a quality that is hard to put into words. For example, you may have broad knowledge across a range of subjects — not deep in any particular subject, but not shallow either. The word 'generalist' falls short. What could work here is a metaphor. Rather than a deep-sea diver, you could describe yourself as a snorkeler in the sea of knowledge.
- Sex up the words. You have the words, but they just don't sound sexy. Find new ways of saying the same thing. Compare 'curious about people' with 'people-watching Olympian'.
- Kill your darlings. Are you over attached to one element in your statement? There might be no way of sexing up

'I like reading leadership books in my leisure time'. So let it go. Tough, I know. You can use it in other settings in your professional life, just not here in your X factor statement.
- Be curious, not serious. Are you taking yourself and the exercises too seriously? If you are stuck, it could be because you are too earnest and hustling with your head. Get over yourself! Time to drop into your heart and have fun with your statement. Instead of pushing for an answer, be curious about what is possible. You need a light, playful touch to succeed.

Dial a friend

Compose your X factor statement. Speak it out aloud. Run it past a trusted mentor. My first 100 readers are invited to email me your top three versions at **support@yamininaidu.com.au**. I promise I will come back with love and advice.

Why am I offering you this? My clients tell me this is exactly the moment when they run up against their inner demons. It's like a speed hump on a well-travelled road that everyone must negotiate. You may think your X factor statements aren't ready to be shared. They're not perfect. Unless you're landing a plane or saving lives, perfectionism is often the enemy of execution.

I'm not giving you a mandate to produce shoddy work or anything you're not proud of. But clutching your work to your heart as you tinker away, crafting and recrafting it, unwilling to share it until it's 'perfect', is a fool's game. In their bestseller *Rework,* authors Jason Fried and David Heinemeier Hansson say it best: 'You still want to make something great. The best way to get there is through iterations.' I hope this allows you the grace to move forward with your X factor statement. If not, what I'm going to say next will put a rocket under the most recalcitrant of bums.

Imagine you're sitting on something good (not perfect) and don't get to market with it first. Guess what? Someone else will. You could have been the first salsa-dancing kombucha brewing artificial intelligence wizard in the world. In fact, you have this exact statement on a bright yellow sticky note on your fridge door. But you hesitated and, lo and behold, someone else claimed this spot.

Even worse, 'someone else' turns out to be an insufferable competitor who has been snapping at your heels for years. Cue gnashing of teeth, beating of chest and loud wailing. Now if you claim something similar as your X factor, it looks like a pale imitation, doesn't it? Who was the second person to walk on the moon again? Budd, Buzz, Beau? Did you have to Google it? The world is teeming with people who cry out in anguish when a good idea hits, claiming, 'Oh, but I thought of that first'. Yes, but you did nothing with it. Please don't let that be you.

BREAKING THE RULES

So far, I have been manically prescriptive about not using any business or professional terms in your X factor statement. You might look at my statement and say, hey, you're talking about being an economist and a storyteller, which includes some of your professional qualities. Are you playing by different rules? No, but I know when to break the rules.

My X factor has evolved and in writing this book I am considering whether to continue to keep it so professionally focused. An X factor statement does and should evolve and deepen over time. My professional claims are also pretty rare. According to Australian Government National

Skills Commission data in 2021–22 there are only 7,500 economists in Australia. Business storyteller has become known as a profession only in the past decade. It was a qualification that I claimed quite early and that hasn't been widely claimed since. Also, my statement is so crazy that it works!

Remember, this process is an art, so once you know the rules you can break them. I am going to allow you some leeway now to bring in *one professional word*. You're welcome! You can shave off the last word on your statement and replace it with a business word. BUT (aha, new rules) only if:

- the word is **NOT listed** on my *100+ Banned X factor words* list. Using a banned word, will make your X factor statement self-destruct.
- the word is **uncommon** (think *ideas launcher, pattern detective* or *business blacksmith*).
- you already have **two strong elements** in your X factor statement. I cannot stress this enough: the business word needs to be anchored by two strong personal words to work. Otherwise, the business word will make the whole statement collapse.

If in doubt, leave it out. If you're not sure, please don't introduce a business word; 99% of statements work like magic because they don't include any business words.

Here's a case study that pulls all this together.

CASE STUDY
GOLD STAR X FACTOR STATEMENT

Tracey Ezard works with leaders and their teams to build dynamic leadership and collaborative learning cultures that create new ways of working in a complex world. Tracey is a keynote speaker, author and educator, and a warm, authentic and wise human being.

As I worked through the process with Tracey, this is the X factor statement that emerged: 'Ex-recorder player, Harley-Davidson bike rider, ferocious warmth leader'.

This is a gold X factor statement. One element is relatable ('ex-recorder player'), one is aspirational ('Harley-Davidson bike rider') and one is inspirational ('ferocious warmth leader'). She breaks the rules with this last word. Here's a breakdown of the three elements of Tracey's statement and why they work.

Element 1 ('ex-recorder player') is funny and relatable. Who isn't an ex-recorder player? But no one thinks to dwell on it. That's what makes it genius. It's an instant, warm idea that will surprise and delight any audience.

Element 2 ('Harley-Davidson bike rider') is aspirational. It sparks desire in us all and provides a surprising contrast to the first element. It immediately restores Tracey's credibility. These are strong sensory words: you can picture them in your imagination.

Element 3 ('ferocious warmth leader'). As her first two elements are so strong, Tracey can break the rule and bring in a professional element. What

> makes it work is that it's Tracey's IP, unique to her. She created the ferocious warmth leadership program and even wrote the book. Finishing here allows her to end her X factor statement with where she wants her audience to meet her now. Inspiring!

How can you share your X factor statement with the world? That's the only way to know what works and what doesn't. Here are some initial ideas. In the chapters that follow I'll look in more detail at how you can use your X factor in your presentations.

PROGRESS BY STEALTH

The earlier you start, and sometimes the smaller you start, the better. This allows elements of your X factor statement to unfold and grow and helps you learn through iteration. This wisdom is timeless, and the ancients were all over it. The Greek poet Hesiod noted way back in 700 BC, 'If you add only a little to a little and do this often, soon that little will become great'.

Can a sip of kombucha launch a comedy career? In 2019 a young Texan woman filmed herself trying kombucha for the first time. She hates it, pulls a face in disgust, then changes her mind, leaning in for another sip with a honking laugh. She posted her reaction on TikTok. It is funny and irresistible and was an instant internet hit. That first sip of kombucha launched the comedy career of Brittany Broski, aka Kombucha Girl, who now has 7 million followers and brand deals (yes with kombucha companies) and has relocated to LA. Do a Brittany and start small and start where you are.

Pick one element of your X factor statement and I will show you shortly how to work it into your next presentation. We will also look at this in detail in the next chapter. No one knows (other than you and me) that you are slowly weaving elements of your X factor statement into your presentations.

This may not be what you want to hear. You would love to launch your X factor with pyrotechnics, a publicity blitz and a world tour. But sometimes, especially so early in your journey, gently and slowly does it best. There are grave dangers in going hell for leather at this stage. In March 2019, entrepreneur Dom Holland launched *Fast*, a one-click tool storing password and payment information. *Fast* raised millions of dollars, but its lacklustre growth resulted in the start-up being abruptly shut down. 'The world's fastest CEO' is how Holland describes himself. 'He may be right: He's in contention for the title of the fastest CEO to ever burn through $100 million in funding,' writers at *The Daily Upside* newsletter observed cuttingly.

Fast and furious is not what you want now. Time to handcuff your hare and channel your inner tortoise and remember that slow and steady wins this race. Fifteen years ago I used Bollywood dancing as an energiser; about seven years ago I used it as a speaking point, and now I use it as a teaching point. But you have compressed the time and space continuum with the work we have done together. I have packed 15 years into 45,000-plus words to help you get there fast but also safely.

Easy does it

Once you have chosen one element from your X factor statement, think about how you can start to use it in your next presentation. What would be the simplest way? What would be the first step, the second step? What would success look like?

For me, the easiest element to showcase was that I am an economist. I know it doesn't sound X factorish, but it is the starting point of my story and anchors everything that follows. I could do complex economic theories or explain the link between inflation and employment using relevant market data or demystify the current federal budget. But only if I wanted my audience to flee screaming for the hills. So I weave this element into my presentation through (are you ready?) a joke about economists! The joke works every time. This element of my X factor statement needs nothing more than that. Too easy? Good. Next.

Butter scraped over too much bread

In Tolkien's *Fellowship of the Ring*, a beleaguered Bilbo Baggins says, 'I feel thin, sort of stretched, like butter scraped over too much bread'. Don't spread yourself too thin at this point, trying too many new things. You'll know someone who, having decided on a fresh start, joins a gym, cuts out junk food, runs 10 km a day, goes great guns for a month ... then drops off the wagon spectacularly. You don't want that.

For now, go with just one element from your X factor statement. Grade the three elements in terms of how easy or hard you think they will be to weave into a presentation. This will be based on your skill level (what is involved), your confidence and your audience, so it is a personal calculation. Here's how I have graded mine.

> *Easy*
>
> World's only **economist** turned **Bollywood-dancing** business **storyteller**
>
> *Hard*
>
> *Medium*

It's easy for me to weave in a joke about economists.

Every story must be tailored and tested for the audience and message, which takes work. But Bollywood dancing, which is done live on stage and involves the audience, is the hardest to carry off as so much can go wrong.

Start with the easiest element and practise using my formula below:

- Keep it simple.
- List the first (small) step you can take to use it in your presentation (more ideas on this in the next chapter).
- List the next steps.
- Think about what success will look like.
- Commit to taking that first step.
- Reflect on the action.
- Iterate and get better each time.

'Just do it' tips

- What is the smallest step you can take to weave one element of your X factor statement into your next presentation? Could it be sharing a small anecdote, using it as a metaphor or sharing a joke?
- What resources (both inner and external) do you have currently that will help you do this?
- What obstacles might you put in your own way to block success? How will you overcome these obstacles?

Healing the world

For a few years I worked out of Hub Melbourne, Australia's first co-working space. Hub's superpower is making work fun. How often do you have fun at work, let alone with your X factor? It doesn't have to be party fun and can be something small.

Dr Prashan Karunaratne is the Course Director of the Bachelor of Commerce at Macquarie Business School. He is an innovative, award-winning teacher of economics and business analytics. Students often think of economics and business subjects as dry, even boring, but Dr Karunaratne uses Disney films to make business and economics fun. He looks at the dynamics of the Disney film *Frozen* to lead a discussion about monopoly markets. Long live inspiring educators like Dr Karunaratne.

'Fun coach' Bernie De Koven believes, 'When fun gets deep enough it can heal the world'. When you start weaving elements of your X factor statement into your presentation, note that you need a playful, light energy to succeed.

I recommend picking something fun, something you love, to make the elements of your X factor statement come alive. When something is fun, you have a natural inclination to share it. It calls out to you. Don't ignore this. But a note of caution: sometimes using something you love in a work context can change its associations. So, choose wisely.

What a roller-coaster ride you've had in Lab You! You've sharpened and deepened your X factor elements and have crafted and recrafted your X factor statement.

You've learned how to get unstuck and when you can break the rules (gasp). You've progressed by stealth (this wins your vote) and accepted the ironclad rule that your X factor must be fun. In the next part you'll learn how to future-proof your X factor by embracing it in your presentations and growing it.

CHAPTER 7

EMBRACE AND SHOWCASE

Poet and activist Amanda Gorman tells us, 'We are the good news that we have been looking for. Demonstrating that every dusk holds a dawn disguised within it. Today we don't burst into a new world. We begin it'.

Let's create this future world.

Now comes the most important part. What will you do next? How can you future-proof your X factor statement? The first step, of course, is to get it out there in the world.

This chapter explores how you can embrace the elements of your X factor statement, whether it's still in development or is fully resolved. It all starts with you. You also learn to do this with humility and by practising five cautions.

Embracing your X factor is an explosive step, as it means 'going live' with your X factor statement or elements of it. This is when you get to reap the rewards of all your hard work. You learn how to unleash this presentation superpower and enthrall any audience. I pack this chapter with tips and ideas, so you can start small or take the world by storm. You choose.

KNOW, OWN, BE KNOWN

Embracing your X factor means knowing it, owning it and being known for it. You must ask yourself these questions: Am I proud of my statement? Does it represent me? Would I be happy if people recognised me by my X factor? Keynote speaker Judson Laipply, who we first met in chapter 2, uses dance as a metaphor for change. Many people refer to him as 'that evolution of dance guy'.

Embracing your X factor statement in its entirety is a confidence move. You've done the work, out of which was born an X factor statement containing at least three elements. This is all you need at this point. If you have several X factor statements, choose one. Later you can work with your other statements as well, but right now make a start with just one.

How do you know the one you choose is the right one? You don't. But don't think of this as a permanent, irreversible decision. Think of it as the first iteration of your X factor statement, the bottom rung on the ladder. There may be many more iterations to come. Here's a snapshot view of my journey to embrace my X factor:

business storyteller
↓
world's only economist turned business storyteller
↓
world's only economist turned
Bollywood-dancing business storyteller.

Retrospectively, it looks like I went through distinct phases, with a plan and a staged embracing of my X factor.

Nothing could be further from the truth. It all started with taking that first step 15 years ago, embracing the identity of business storyteller, giving myself permission to own that and be that. At the time, that felt like a huge step. I had to grow into my X factor, and that growth wouldn't have been possible without my taking that first step.

The Persian poet Rumi says, 'As you start to walk on the way, the way appears'. Your baby X factor, as you tend it, nurture it, embrace it, will become fully fledged. When you know and own it, the next step in the process will reveal itself.

SMALL DOORS

Share your X factor by starting small. Small doors can lead to big opportunities. Consider the example of Brittany Broski, 'Kombucha Girl', shared in the previous chapter. You choose how you are going to showcase this baby X factor. Remember, nothing you do is set in stone and you can change it as you grow deeper into your X factor. Here are some simple ideas on how to get going:

1. Add your X factor statement to your bio.
2. Introduce yourself with one of your X factor elements or your whole statement.
3. Write up different versions for each social media platform on which you have a presence — Twitter, YouTube, Instagram.
4. Spark curiosity, connection, and change. When Carolyn Tate introduces herself as a river swimmer, people's eyes light up, they ask lots of questions and she soon finds herself welcoming a new member to her river swimming community.

5. Draw on it in any context as your magic answer to the 'So what do you do?' question.
6. Add it to your Master of Ceremonies introduction blurb.
7. Use it at dinner parties when you tire of small talk and discussing price rises.
8. Update your dating bio!

Note that your X factor statement doesn't work in your LinkedIn profile, which will usually be more pragmatic. Your 'About me' section on LinkedIn is about your audience and what you can do for them.

Owning and being known for your X factor can only begin when you share it with the world. You don't have to use the term itself; in fact, it's better not to. Just incorporate it in what you do, how you show up and, therefore, what others write about you.

Sharing your X factor statement opens the door to a world of possibility. Which is why even a baby X factor needs to be given light, air and love by sharing it with the world. Share it in whatever way works for you. You don't have to make a song and dance about it, but you must do it. Every time you're asked to give a presentation, seize the opportunity to showcase your X factor. Start small, start where you are and start today.

X FACTOR IN YOUR NEXT PRESENTATION

Lisa Leong is a broadcaster, author and interviewer. I worked with Lisa on her TEDx Melbourne talk titled, 'Can robots make us more human?'. Based on my professional advice she performed some rap for one of her messages. Pure X factor.

The first time anyone had heard of a rapping lawyer. (Yes, she's a lawyer too.)

To introduce any of your X factor elements into your next presentation, like Lisa, work with your key messages. If you haven't refined your key messages yet, revisit chapter 3. Here's a high-level process overview for introducing X factor into presentations, followed by some examples of how to do it well.

1. Highlight a key message from your presentation.
2. It must be a message you want your audience to understand, remember and retell.
3. Highlight one word from your X factor statement.
4. Now look carefully at both your key message and your X factor statement.
5. How can your X factor best serve your audience and this message?
6. Put your thinking cap on and give yourself permission to start small. Think laterally.
7. If it's not clicking, move to another word in your statement.
8. Ask a trusted friend or colleague for their advice on how to incorporate your X factor. (Or ask me via email — it's my job *he he!*)
9. Move to a new message, rinse and repeat.
10. Experiment with a few options.
11. Road test for a small audience.
12. Practise, then showtime.

Figure 7.1 High-level overview for introducing X factor into presentations

This is how the process works for me. The three highlighted words in my X factor statement are *economist*, *storyteller* and *Bollywood-dancing*.

World's only **economist**
turned **Bollywood-dancing**
business **storyteller**

I look at a key message and think, is there a theory in economics I can apply? In chapter 1 my message was that 10% X factor is non-negotiable. I used reference point theory from behavioural economics to make the point. For the same message I also added the story of the Olympic medal winners to make the theory come alive. I would do a simplified version of this theory and story in a presentation.

If I use Bollywood dancing in my presentation, I use it only once. I choose a message I want my audience to remember when they are back at work. In this context, dance is based on the principle of kinaesthetic learning, using movement and physical activity to anchor knowledge. I teach a Bollywood move and tie it to a keyword.

I use only three moves and three keywords. For example, one of my messages is: '*In business your stories must have a purpose, support data and be authentic*'. For each of those keywords: purpose, data and authentic, I teach my audience a Bollywood move. Three words, three different moves to help remember the words.

The moves are simple and anyone can do them, sitting if it's virtual or standing if we are face to face. Then we dance it out. The whole exercise takes less than two minutes and can create several moments of laughter, fun and connection and, most importantly, aid recall of the messages. I track its success through formal evaluation and feedback, rebookings and recommendations.

Let's explore this process and some examples of how to apply it. I share examples below to show how X factor has limitless potential to transform how your audience experiences your presentation.

I'll explore three ways in which you can use your X factor in your next presentation:

1. Nailing a point
2. Participatory X factor
3. Performative X factor.

This is a hierarchy, and you must do this in the order listed. The order sets you up for success. Start with nailing a point and then participatory X factor, both explained below. In the next chapter you will explore performative X factor, an advanced ninja move.

Nailing a point

When noting a point, you make a bald statement that your audience is unlikely to remember. When *nailing* a point, however, you apply your X factor, or an element of your X factor statement, to make the same message marvellous and memorable. Here's an example.

One of my messages is that as professionals you are not afraid of hard work. This is true but bland, ho hum. I have recently been playing with using different kinds of dance moves (not just Bollywood) in my presentations. This is how I have X factored this message.

Some context: In the early nineties, the British group Right Said Fred (aka the Fairbrass brothers) had a hit single called 'I'm Too Sexy for My Shirt'. If you haven't heard of it, I commend you on your good taste. If you have heard it, just remembering that title will have set off an ear worm in your head. My apologies. The Fairbrass brothers ran a gym in London. In the gym there was a lot of posing, as people admired themselves in the wall mirrors. While doing just that, as a joke, one brother took off his shirt and sang 'I'm too sexy for my shirt'. And the hit single was born.

This is how I use this in my presentation.

Message: Business professionals are not afraid of hard work.
Audience: Business professionals.

Script (what I say)	What I do
I moved to Australia in the early 1990s. Remember the 1990s?	Raise my hand, inviting audience members to do the same
High-waisted ripped jeans, the internet made a noise…	Play sound of modem connecting to internet
and this hit single by British group Right Said Fred…	Play licensed music here (first lines of the chorus) and dance to it – invite audience to do the same
While we might be too sexy for our shirts, as professionals we are never too sexy for the work.	Link to message

Which message in your presentation can you supercharge by applying your X factor to it? If funny storytelling is one of your X factors, how can you make one of your messages pop by linking it to a suitable funny story or appropriate joke?

Start by picking the easiest messages. Don't make it hard on yourself. Go slow now to go fast later. If it's too hard to do all three elements, pick just one word from your X factor statement. Remember Sandy McDonald, the story whisperer, and her X factor statement: 'Zimbabwean-born, cloud-obsessed, orchid cacti cultivator'. The easiest place for Sandy to start was to share a story from her childhood in Zimbabwe. She chose a story that served her *message* and her *audience*. These are the two touchstones you must always come back to.

Anything you do will be a step up, fresh. Even one micro action today is a start. **When you X factor a message, you're not just noting the message, you're** nailing **it for your audience.**

Participatory X factor

This is a level up for your X factor: Participatory X factor is involving your audience to create the magic. This is when you do your X factor *with* your audience, not *to* them. Reader warning: the example I share here is aspirational, to show what is possible.

CASE STUDY
WINNING WORDS

Lisa McInnes Smith, CSP, is in the top 3 % of keynote speakers in the world. Her website states that she has authored seven bestselling books, spoken to over 2.5 million adults across 28 countries, and shared the stage with two American presidents and a host of celebrities.

In her TEDx Melbourne talk, 'Winning Words! The Phrases That Pay', Lisa makes a point about changing the words we use to speak to ourselves: she says the only way to change these words is through training.

Lisa then invites her audience to stand up and to bend their knees to 45 degrees. She then says, 'This is a fantastic position for learning environments. You cannot fall asleep in this position. And what this position is called is ... *pain*'. The audience is doing exactly what she says and is laughing. She now invites them to bend their knees further, to go 10% beyond pain. She says, 'This position is called *agony*.' Coming back up to the first position she asks her audience, 'Isn't pain easy after agony?' By now the audience is groaning and roaring with laughter. She then invites them to sit back down.

I highly recommend checking out her talk. It is participatory X factor mastery in action.

As you start challenging yourself on how to involve your audience, what is possible grows. It's like letting the genie out of the bottle. Any wish can come true!

Involving the audience immediately lifts the energy and the entertainment factor and creates a wow moment. But it's not easy.

Success tips

You need to be confident in leading audience involvement. Give simple instructions. Make it easy for everyone to succeed. No one will take part if they think they might fail or look foolish.

You must stay in control of this activity. Give your audience explicit instructions on the finish line and what to do once the activity is complete. This stops people from lingering and chatting.

Any audience involvement must be 100% safe. Not just physically safe, but psychologically safe. This means your audience need to feel confident they can do what you ask them to, that everyone will participate, that they won't feel silly and won't be judged. As a presenter, you create psychological safety by building to this level of trust. Start small by asking for a show of hands to get them warmed up. Each time, ask for a little more from your audience. After a show of hands, you could prompt them to chat to the person next to them. For one of your points, you could ask if your audience has an example they'd like to share.

Warmly acknowledge every response. Each time you do this you are reassuring your audience that it is safe to contribute, that this is a safe space where they are respected. All this makes your audience feel psychologically safe.

Always thank and reward your audience with a round of applause just for them, praising even the shakiest of efforts. Honour and respect every effort. It takes adults a lot of courage to put themselves out there.

How else can you grow and future-proof your X factor? Welcome to the world of 'edge work'. You may already live there or at least be familiar with it.

EDGE WORK

Raise your hand if you had never given a virtual presentation prior to 2019. That would be true of most business professionals. And look at you now. You are presenting across platforms, virtually and online, without blinking an eye. Tearing your hair out when technology fails is optional. Looking back, I feel nostalgic for the early days of Zoom. Like pioneers, we grappled with bad lighting, the mute button and Zoom bombing.

The pandemic precipitated this change, but you were already presenting face to face, so virtual presenting was on the edge of your expertise. Sometimes your X factor will come out of your edge work. Sociology defines edge work as behaviour at the boundary of what is normally accepted.

Corey Baker is a New Zealand–born classical and contemporary choreographer, film director and former dancer. As a quarantine project, Baker directed, choreographed and remotely filmed 27 elite ballet dancers from all over the world performing a modern-day Swan Lake in their bathtubs. 'Swan Lake in a bathtub' became a viral hit. It is a classic example of edge work, pushing against convention.

Edge work involves both skill and risk taking. The risk-taking means edge work engages emotions such as fear and excitement, both for you and for your audience. Edge work is not for the fainthearted, but it's supercharged with possibilities. Remember, you are experimenting, so nothing is off limits.

How can you find your edge? With your interlinking circles that you completed in chapter 5, extend lines out of the most promising circles, or each circle as shown in figure 7.2. Write an extreme version of what each X factor word or phrase might look like. Go crazy, go wild, go nuts. This is the time to channel a Cirque du Soleil performer. Would it be remembering people's names while hanging upside down from a trapeze? I've provided more examples below. **It is in areas outside your expertise that you will find your edge.** Over time this could become your X factor.

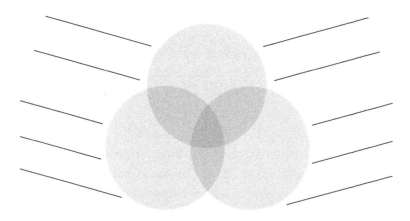

Figure 7.2 Extended interlinking circles

Here's an example of my extended interlinked circles. I've explored possible ways I could extend two of my X factor elements.

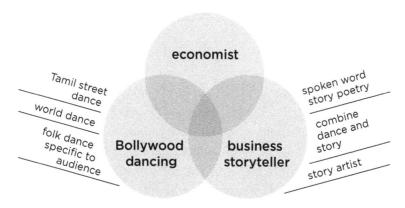

Figure 7.3 Extended interlinking circles example

Building on her interlinking circles, book coach Kath Walters started with 'cycle path nerd' and ended up with sharing her ultimate dream of a six-lane cycle freeway. Sandy McDonald grew from 'cloud-obsessed' to becoming a drone so she could live in the clouds. Carolyn Tate morphed from 'river-swimming' to living in the river. This is the time to let your imagination go wild.

You are mapping the future evolution of your X factor. Who knows, this evolution might trigger a revolution. Poet and singer-songwriter Sampa the Great (Sampa Tembo) says, 'Change is how we grow'. Sampa was born in Zambia and moved to Australia when she was 22 years old. Her music mixes spoken word and pure hip-hop rapping with psychedelia and blues. In her TEDx Melbourne performance she said, 'It wasn't fists in the air, it was looking in the mirror and loving my hair. Revolution is sometimes in here [she points to her heart]'.

Revolution starts with you.

The bold and the beautiful

Take another look at your extended interlinking circles. Can you start to bring any of these into your work? Perhaps they represent the fully resolved version of what is possible. Moving out from the centre of a circle, what is the simplest step you can take? Think of building a ladder, with an action for each step that would help you extend your X factor out. Whatever you do, make it your own and have fun with it.

Remember how Judson Laipply made his original evolution of dance video, rocking out to 12 popular dances from the past 50 years, in 2001 and uploaded a three-minute clip to YouTube a few years later. His 'Evolution of Dance 2' video was part of a national viral marketing campaign. He produced 'Evolution of Dance 3' to mark the 10-year anniversary of his first video. Laipply has appeared in advertisements for the BBC and featured in dance videos and in YouTube's annual Rewind, which recaps each year's viral videos, events, trends and music. His X factor keeps on giving, but only because he deliberately grows it with new iterations and collaborations on his tested formula.

What new skills do you need to extend your X factor? How can you make your X factor more layered? Looking for new opportunities to grow your X factor is like standing in a fast-flowing stream. Keep one foot firmly on a rock (your current X factor) then reach out with your other foot to search for the next rock. The same applies to future-proofing your X factor. Keep doing what you do, but never stop thinking about how you could extend it, making it bolder and more beautiful.

Here are some further tips for extending the exercise you did on your history, hobbies and (h)interesting facts in chapter 5. You can also use this to create extensions on your interlinking circles.

Start collecting your personal stories, as if you're writing your autobiography.
Ask your parents and grandparents more about their lives and childhoods.
Pretend you're featuring in the TV series *Who Do You Think You Are?* and trace your family's story and lineage.
Ask about and explore your friends' hobbies, interests and passions. This could spark some ideas for you.
Notice what you were doing when time flies.
Make a list of all your favourite things. List everything, no matter how small.
What lights you up? Think about how you could use this in your next presentation.
What makes your chest buoyant? What makes your chest constrict? List them.
Add something new to this list.

Figure 7.4: Extension exercise

Next, I'll consider some important cautions that keep you and your X factor safe.

LIGHTNING IN A BOTTLE

Leave your ego at the door. For your X factor to be successful, you must stay humble. It may sound new agey, but after a decade working at the coal face of senior leadership, I know this to be true. It is one field where doubt can be your friend, a fierce friend.

Who are you to share your X factor with the world? Staying in touch with doubt will keep your X factor humble. Rather than the arrogant conviction that everyone is dying to experience your X factor, humility is the best starting place for success. Feel the doubt but press on anyway and learn from each experience. The doubt will keep your ideas grounded and remind you to practise and prepare. Putting your X factor out in the world will give you the experience you need to get better each time.

Now I'll look at specific cautions you must take with your X factor. Why? Because X factor is like lightning in a bottle. Once unleashed, you can't always control it.

Abhyāsa

Abhyāsa, is a Sanskrit word meaning 'practice'. Show up and complete all the steps I've shown you. It may be unexciting, unsexy advice, but no matter how gifted, quick thinking and spontaneous you are, you will *always* do better if you are well prepared.

Your X factor needs preparation, practice and more preparation. There are three essentials to practising abhyasa: practising without interruption, practising for a longer time, and remaining committed to the practice even when things are tough.

Abhyāsa is how you get confident with your X factor. It

grows and solidifies because you invest in it. It ensures your X factor appears effortless.

Abhyāsa lets you roll with the punches on the day of your presentation, accepting that sometimes stuff goes wrong. The better prepared you are, the better you will deal with any such curveball thrown your way in a live presentation. If you are already stumbling and hesitant, any glitch can tip you over the edge.

Vairagya

Despite all your preparation, unleashing your X factor can still be risky and sometimes messy. You may be an excellent driver, but you can't always control the driving conditions or the recklessness of other drivers.

While Abhyāsa prepares you, Vairagya frees you to act. Another Sanskrit word, Vairagya means non-attachment to the outcomes. It frees you from the possible disappointment of your expectations. X factor is like doing your best comedy set at one in the morning in a club full of drunk patrons, who talk over your best jokes. It's your best work, but you cannot control the outcome. Understanding this is a key to X factor success. Do your best and leave the rest.

Without Vairagya, you might be too embarrassed or scared to take a risk and try out your X factor; or you might try once, fall flat and never try again. Recently, I was looking at some conference footage. I am up on enormous screens in the conference, leading some dancing. The entire audience is up and dancing, and there I am dancing the whole time with my mouth wide open! My partner asked helpfully, 'Why do you always dance with your mouth open?' So embarrassing. Then I thought of embracing Vairagya. The audience loved it, were all up and dancing, and the formal feedback was terrific. I have, though, now learned to dance with my mouth shut.

Too much salt

X factor is like seasoning on a dish. Too much salt can kill the best food. Don't overdo it. It's tempting, especially when you have just discovered your X factor, to paper it all over your presentation. Why sing one song when you can sing three? Why attach one funny story to one message? Let's make the whole thing a laugh fest. Resist this temptation. No matter how brilliant it is, overdoing it is not a good idea. In his podcast *Steal the Show*, bestselling author, co-founder and CEO of Heroic Public Speaking, Michael Port, shares this feedback one speaker received from an audience member: 'If I wanted to laugh nonstop, I would have gone to a comedy show not come here.' Ouch.

When you overdo your X factor, it's exhausting for your audience. Your entire presentation is in a high key. Nothing will stand out or feel special. The contrasts, the 'white space', the shades of grey all matter for your X factor to shine. Think of your last visit to an art gallery. Remember how the art was spaced out on the walls, each work beautifully lit and thoughtfully positioned. It isn't all crowded onto one wall or just flung there like a Jackson Pollock painting, all blobs and dribbles. This allows each artwork to shine and hold its own. You need to do the same with your X factor.

Less is best

A well-known principle in economics is the law of diminishing returns. Simply put, it means that after a certain point, the more you invest in something the less you get back. What this suggests for your X factor is that you would be wise to stop sooner than you might be tempted to. Sing the first verse and the chorus, perhaps, rather than the whole song.

If you are doing a magic trick or leading any activity, for example, run it tight. Even if you showcase your X factor only once in the entire presentation, this rule still applies. Less is best.

End before your audience is quite ready, leaving your audience wanting more. It sets the stage for an encore. Who knows? Your X factor creates peak experiences in your presentation, but if it goes on for too long, there's a risk that your audience will feel short-changed on other parts of your presentation.

BS detectors

A few years ago at a conference I led the audience through some Bollywood dancing. When I finished up, the MC said, probably reflecting what the room was thinking, 'Yamini, when you started, I had a moment of doubt because I thought isn't this cultural appropriation? And I thought no — because you are leading it'.

Your X factor must be authentic. Research suggests that Australian audiences have especially active BS detectors. Your X factor can't be contrived, manufactured or appropriated.

We live in a world with a fierce cancel culture, and our audiences are sensitive about cultural appropriation. You must focus your effort on your history, your hobbies and your (h)interesting facts to establish your X factor's provenance. There's a rule in both comedy and storytelling, which I suggest applies equally to X factor: *If it's personal, it can't be wrong.*

Once you've made even a humble start with your X factor, there's no turning back. You must keep developing it, growing it and future-proofing it. More on this in the following chapter.

Actor, comedian and podcaster Cameron Esposito says, 'There is no formula for success — you just begin and then you continue … the answer is confoundingly simple: Do the work. Over and over again, just do the work. After you build the courage to get onstage that first time, it's all about repetition.'

Once you embrace your X factor and grow in your confidence and practice, you are ready for the next phase, evolving and future-proofing, which is what we'll look at next.

CHAPTER 8

EVOLVE AND BE FUTURE READY

For presenters the tides are rising quickly. Even nuns have discovered TikTok. So over time you need to extend your X factor. This can happen only once you are seasoned. As your confidence grows, people trust you more and you trust yourself more. Time does some heavy lifting for you.

Evolution ensures your X factor isn't frozen for 36 years like actor Tom Cruise's face seems to be, essentially unchanged since the first Top Gun movie. In this chapter I share some life-changing secrets on how you can continue to grow, serve and impress your audience. Your mission, should you choose to accept it ...

PERFORMATIVE X FACTOR

Goosebumps, tears, a standing ovation. This was the audience response to the spoken word poetry shared by Darren Hill, behavioural scientist, and Co-Founder of three-time AFR

Fast 100 company Pragmatic Thinking, at the 2018 Future of Leadership Conference.

This is an example of performative X factor, where the presenter uses a specific talent, skill or gift to help land some messages. A performative X factor takes your audience on a journey that is both unexpected and exciting. It is a practice often used by professionals who speak for a living. Speaking is their full-time job. But anyone who presents can learn how.

A performative X factor is worth its weight in gold because it creates unforgettable magic for your audience. Amanda Gore is one of Australia's and America's best keynote speakers, an author, *Huffington Post* columnist and businesswoman. She is one of just four Australians inducted into the US Speaker Hall of Fame. In one of her presentations Amanda had people dancing in the aisles across broadcast locations several states apart! This happened in 2013, and I still meet people today who remember the event. Be aware, then, that though it's a high-stakes game, the right performative X factor transforms the audience experience and creates lifelong memories. Just as Amanda Gore did.

Finding your rocket fuel

Performative X factor is like rocket fuel. You will be ready for performative X factor *only* after you have had experience in nailing a point and using participatory X factor, both covered in chapter 7. This progression is illustrated in figure 8.1. Moving towards a performative X factor takes time, experience and maturity. The risks are greater but so are the rewards.

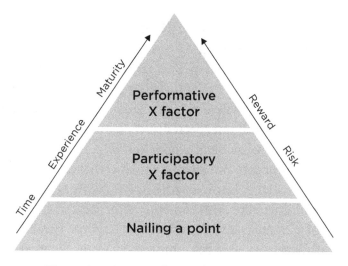

Figure 8.1 Stages of growth of your X factor

You are ready for performative X factor only after you have reached a stage of some maturity in your X factor journey. Never start there. It would be like trying to leap to the top of a ladder without using the intervening steps. Of course, some readers will already have years of performance experience in other areas of their lives, such as on the comedy circuit, in improv theatre or in the national sword-swallowing championship. If this is you, then you can move forward on this journey more quickly, as you are already a seasoned performer.

Performative X factor offers unlimited possibilities. Imagine rewriting the words to a popular song using messages from your presentation, or playing your guitar and having the audience sing a chorus with you. There are innumerable variations of this, but they all depend on one thing: having a skill or talent you can share *in service of your message and your audience.* I cannot stress enough that this is what makes a performative X factor work. Otherwise, it's self-indulgent and superfluous. The questions to ask yourself are:

- Do I have a skill or talent I can demonstrate live on stage?
- How can I use this to add a performance element to my X factor?
- How will this serve my audience and message? When I worked at an e-commerce company, we repurposed the lyrics of Gloria Gaynor's hit 'I will survive' as a motivational anthem. Our audience loved it, and the new words reflected the company's journey and hope for the future.
- Am I good enough (not great or the best) at this skill to demo it?
- Have I road-tested this with a paid professional coach or mentor who will provide me with honest feedback?
- Is it safe for me, my audience and the context?
- Am I prepared to rehearse thoroughly?
- Do I have the confidence to pull this off?

The road-testing step with a paid expert is critical to your success. It ensures what you are doing is cool and not cringe. Sadly, recently I saw a presenter perform cringeworthy rap/spoken word poetry. Not even sure what it was, apart from bad. Every member of the audience looked gobsmacked. It was a virtual presentation with cameras on, so you could see the shock on people's faces as they watched. What made it sad was that the presenter was so confident it was super cool. Everyone (me included) must always road-test their performative X factor with an expert who can give honest feedback. It's like a pilot's licence — you wouldn't dream of flying a plane without one. Same goes for your performative X factor. You MUST road-test it with an expert not just your partner, friend or colleague.

X factor is always curated for an audience. Here's a shining example. The best master of ceremonies in the world,

Warwick Merry, CSP, CVP, turns his audience into a choir. Yes, you read that right. He shared this experience in a recent LinkedIn post:

> *'Before we rush into "But that's beyond some people's comfort zone", let me tell you that I specifically chose a song that most people know, I specifically only asked them to sing the chorus, and I even made the song about them. It went so well, some of my clients now request it. Let's be completely honest, the singing is not perfect either, but the joy, energy and memorability are way up there!'*

You've got to love the honesty and insights in that. Here the X factor is curated for the audience, it sets them up for success and it's done *with* them, not *to* them.

Three balls in the air

If no skill, talent or God-given gift magically appears for you, here are some ways to find it now. Make a list of all your talents and skills (even if they're quite rusty). The top 10 talents in *America's Got Talent* are singing, dancing, playing musical instruments, novelty acts, acrobatics, danger acts, comedy and magic acts, animal acts and impressions. This list is a starting place for considering what could work for a performative X factor, but don't let it constrain you.

List only the talents or skills you can show live in a presentation. Pottery, for example, might be a bit too messy and impractical, or downright impossible. The next step is to consider one of your messages, and the audience that you'll be presenting to. Which one of your talents could work for both the message and audience? It's like you have three balls up in the air: talent, message, audience. If your audience is a group of emerging start-ups, they might appreciate some of your messages delivered as slam poetry. But this might go down like poison with a group of conservative bureaucrats. You must check with the event organisers to be safe.

X factor Talent	Message	YES or NO for this audience
Slam poetry	Fortune favours the brave.	Entrepreneurs — YES
Slam poetry	Fortune favours the brave.	Senior bureaucrats — NO (Have checked with the organisers)
Slam poetry	Fortune favours the brave.	Secondary school principals — Not sure, check with organisers

Figure 8.2 Three balls in the air test

If you can marry your X factor talent with your message and your audience, great work — you have won the holy trifecta for a successful performative X factor. You'll no longer find yourself bursting into song at random in a desperate effort to lift an uninspiring performance. Instead, you'll have chosen carefully to sing some of your content only once you're convinced it will serve both your message and your audience.

Look at the X factor statement you came up with in chapter 6. Can this talent or skill be added to the mix or can you replace one of the elements? For about a decade my X factor statement was 'The world's only economist turned business storyteller'. I then added the Bollywood-dancing element.

Chase the emotion

If you feel completely bereft of any talents or skills that you can showcase for a live audience, please don't lose hope. There is another path for you. The question to ask is not how can you learn to juggle in 30 days but how can you bring more joy, connection, laughter into your presentation. As your starting point, clarify what positive emotion you want more of in your presentation, then work out if there is a talent you can use to serve this emotion.

If you are going to be using your performative X factor, there are some points to note. You must always, always check with the event organisers, a trusted mentor or a target audience member if they think this will be okay. Listen to their advice and take it on board, even if it's not what you want to hear. You may be busting to perform, but that doesn't mean this audience is dying to experience it. **A performative X factor is not something to pull out every time, everywhere for every audience. It is curated, considered and context specific.**

A performative X factor needs 10,000-plus hours of practice. Warwick Merry sings in a choir every week and has done for years. You don't need to be the Bob Dylan of the business world to use song, but you do need to be reasonably good at it. Good enough to pull it off, sing in tune, hold an audience. And you'll have practised so much it hurts. That's why so few people attempt it. You need to be good (not great or the best) and well prepared.

A performative X factor takes oversized courage. When you're ready, I invite you to embrace the spirit of action with your performative X factor, knowing that action brings the fruit of rewards.

OXYGEN LANGARS

'Instapoet' Rupi Kaur posts reels and photos of her typewritten poems. Kaur has repurposed her traditionally analogue written poetry on social media platforms, gaining a global audience, cult status and book deals.

You may think you have to invent something from scratch, which is hard. Consider, instead, how you might reinvent what you already have, do or are as part of your future-proofing. Think how many modern adaptations of Jane Austen's classic *Pride and Prejudice* you may have seen. Among the best known are the movies *Clueless*, *Bridget Jones's Diary* and *Bride and Prejudice*. And just when you thought that trope had been exhausted, comedian and writer Joel Kim Booster gives us *Fire Island*, which recreates Austen's courtship dramas in a vacation hideaway for gay men.

You may already have an X factor statement nailed, then the context changes. You consider how to repurpose your X factor to serve in this new context, as the Sikh community in India did.

Every Indian student knows that no matter where they are in the world, or what day of the week it is, they will always find a free hot, delicious meal at their local *gurdwara*. This is a Sikh place of worship open to people of all faiths. Guru Nanak, the founder of Sikhism, introduced the langar (or free kitchen), which offers free meals to everyone, regardless of their religion, gender or wealth. Volunteers run the langar. They consider it a privilege to help with the cooking, cleaning and serving. There is also a waiting list of people who want to provide food for the langar each week.

When Covid hit India in May 2021, there was a severe shortage of oxygen cylinders. Patients in desperate need of oxygen could not find either oxygen cylinders or a hospital bed. This is when many Sikh temples stepped up to help through an initiative called 'Oxygen Langar'. Just like any langar organised by the Sikh community, the oxygen langar was based on the philosophy of *Sevā* or selfless service. The gurdwaras are already set up to accommodate large numbers of people. These temples now created facilities where patients could use the oxygen available for free. The oxygen langars are credited with saving thousands of lives.

You can repurpose and adapt your X factor to serve any context. X factor is not solid and stiff, like ice, with all the molecules stuck together tightly, or like gas, with the molecules able to fly off in every direction. Rather, it's like water, where the molecules are formed together, but not tightly, allowing water to flow freely, constantly changing its shape to fit the space available.

One of my clients has a deep, sonorous voice and will often belt out a tune or two for his audience, always curated around his message. One time he brought a concern to me. He was presenting to the same audience over two days and didn't want to sing for them again, even though the message was different. So I repurposed the use of his voice, creating a 'podcast moment'. He invited the audience to shut their eyes and listen to him for 60 seconds as he read out a favourite passage from a book. They melted into the words, with his voice guiding them. The passage was picked to tie in with his message and worked like a charm.

The beauty of your X factor is it can always be repurposed, because of its flexible, fluid quality.

SHOWCASE YOUR UGLIES

Your X factor can emerge from darker places; it can live in the shadows. It is then how you package and present it. This is a sure-fire way to future-proof your X factor.

This is a ninja move. I won't lie to you. It's hard to do and even harder to do well, which is why businesspeople often make the mistake of sugar-coating the ugly stuff. An example of a dark X factor is sharing a challenging story. A dark story works well if it has an uplifting ending, or at least a suggestion of light at the end of the tunnel. I do not mean a business version of film noir. You don't want to follow a dark start with dark deeds and a devastating ending, leaving your audience despondent. Handcuff your inner Jean-Luc Godard. One of my clients began with, 'Yesterday we received a customer complaint'.

Yes, that's dark for business. They immediately had everyone's attention. They then talked about how one team member had stayed behind to work on the issue and resolve it. My client finished with a slide that shared the glowing customer thank you email.

A dark X factor must follow an upward trajectory. Finish on a high. The contrast should be strong. **Take your audience from a dark place and leave them dazzled by the light of hope and optimism.**

One key to showcasing your uglies is to share from scars, not the wounds. What these wise words remind us of is not to share anything if it's still a raw, bleeding wound that you haven't processed and learned from. Sharing from a scar, a wound that has healed and scabbed over, is safe for both you and your audience. If done well.

Comedy equals tragedy plus time. These words are often attributed to Mark Twain. Talented comedians can take catastrophic life events and turn them into comedy gold. Sharing from scars shows your audience you aren't broken by a tough experience but are perhaps wiser or, if you're a comic, funnier.

My father passed away suddenly in 2006. It was a shock, and a sad and traumatic time for my family. It wasn't until

2018 that I started sharing stories about him. It took me that long. There's no single answer to when scar tissue forms over your emotional wounds. It's personal and different for everyone. You make that call. And, if you aren't comfortable going there, *don't*. This is not a call to arms for you to have your audience weeping buckets and using this process as group therapy. If it's not for you, sweep it off the table, or revisit it when you're ready. There are many other rich and rewarding sources you can explore to find your X factor.

Just do it tips

- Don't choose a 'faux ugly' line, like the interview candidate who, when asked for his weaknesses, says, 'Oh, I'm a perfectionist'. Right. Next. No, it's got to be real, not fishing for compliments — that's just annoying and twee.
- Don't fake it. Don't call attention to 'weaknesses' that exist only in your imagination. A presenter might apologise for their accent when the audience is thinking, what accent?
- Think of how you can rename something to make it appeal to your audience. For example, in the Argyle diamond mines in Australia, the diamonds mined were all brown. However customers only want white diamonds, known as Champagne diamonds. Urban legend has it that the global advertising company Saatchi & Saatchi came up with the idea of calling brown diamonds … Cognac. So diamonds range from Champagne to Cognac. Genius.
- Sometimes it's okay to admit to an undeniable negative and acknowledge it (audiences love honesty). Oliver Burkeman, author of *The*

Antidote: Happiness for People Who Can't Stand Positive Thinking and *Help! How to Become Slightly Happier and Get a Bit More Done*, calls his newsletter The Imperfectionist. He also admits he is a recovering perfectionist. This is endearing and relatable for his audience.

UNLOCK MAGIC

Can three comedians create a sci-fi show? Comedians Ryan Beil, Maddy Kelly and Mark Chavez set out to do just that, and they made a podcast about their experience. Just when you thought the world had no room for one more podcast, up pops this one, *Let's Make a Sci-Fi*.

The podcast features these three comedians writing a sci-fi script together, consulting and working with diverse people along the way. What makes it easy, entertaining and a standout are the three hosts. They are serious and funny, nerdy and raw, sharing painful lessons along the way. Their co-creation creates magic. And there's a happy ending: in the last episode we listen to professional actors doing a table read of the pilot script.

Co-creation is an advanced karate master move. It's not for the fainthearted, but I highly recommend it. Can you collaborate with someone, with both of you showcasing your X factors in a way that works? It takes any presentation to the next level. I worked with two leaders on their Global Leadership roadshow. We created a volleyball-style firing of questions and answers back and forth. It was fast, funny, unexpected. Most of all, it addressed all the elephants in the room and had everyone in the right frame of mind for what came next. This would have been hard for one presenter to pull off, but co-creation by the two leaders made the presentation pop.

Co-creation unlocks magic. Your X factors bumping up against each other can create something special and fabulous. IKEA launched Co-Create IKEA, a digital platform encouraging customers and fans to develop new products. IKEA invest in successful furniture or product design ideas. For designers and talented fans, this platform is an enormous opportunity. For IKEA, co-creation provides product innovation and design insights. This gives IKEA a huge market advantage and builds a loyal customer community. Win–win.

For a co-creation to work, it's best to have a specific project in mind — an upcoming roadshow, forum or presentation, for example. To succeed, there must be high levels of trust and motivation. There are also the practical aspects, like putting aside enough time and making the preparation and practice a priority, as this process takes longer than working solo. As this wise African proverb reminds us, 'If you want to go fast, go alone; if you want to go far, go together'. There will be road bumps, a clash of ideas and even bruised egos, but what you end up with is usually worth the pain, and you wouldn't have unlocked this magic on your own.

NO MUD, NO LOTUS

My sister and I were sharing memories of our school art classes. She recalled how the teacher often flung her art book out of the window. I was aghast because my sister is good at art. She clarified that the kids who were bad at art frequently had their books torn up and flung out of the window. I'm sure I was one of those kids, but it evidently did me no permanent damage, because I recently enrolled in adult drawing classes.

Every week when I show up at my class I grapple with 'being comfortable being miserable'. This cutting truth nugget is from Steven Pressfield, author of *The War of Art*. 'Miserable' really captures it: the frustration, the temptation to give up and the ghastly comparison-itis.

What surprised me was when the boredom set in. International bestselling author Yuval Harari's recent podcast interview helped me figure out why. Harari explains how it's harder to deal with the subtle pain of boredom than the heroic pain of, say, an artistic crisis. Boredom is the shadow side of the practice that learning requires. More than anything, boredom can break you. It's an abstract pain that sees us reel back from the job at hand and immerse ourselves in distractions.

So why stick with learning? I've been ruminating on this week after week, as I gird my loins for yet another class. I've found some strategies that help. The slightest sense of progress releases a breath of wind under a flailing learner's wings. A good teacher can really help. My art teacher is encouraging and kind, yet honest. She will point out the smallest improvement you have made.

It's also important to shift the story in your head. Too many of us fixate on the perceived truth of statements like 'I'm bad at art' or 'I'm bad at accounts'. I discovered a silver bullet for this from my humour coach, the amazing Kate Burr, who advised: replace 'I am bad at ...' with 'I am learning to be ...'

So your new mantra is 'I'm learning to be good at my X factor.' Affirmations framed by *I am learning* are both gentle and believable to your subconscious mind. This is where the levers need to turn to recalibrate your self-limiting stories.

In the end what makes the difference is deep practice. Not the oversimplification of 10,000 hours of practice, but deliberate, focused practice in chunks. Deliberate practice is getting good at being bad. It's channelling your inner Wile E. Coyote.

The running gag from *Looney Tunes* involves Coyote dropping off a high cliff. We have a bird's-eye view of him disappearing into a canyon so deep we lose sight of him, then seconds later a rising dust cloud signals he has hit the canyon floor. But Wile E. Coyote always lives to see another day and another madcap adventure. Deliberate practice can feel like this: your ego smashed to shards repeatedly, but you never give up the relentless pursuit.

As the late Buddhist teacher Thich Nhat Hanh said, 'No mud, no lotus.' Growing your X factor may require you to wallow in the mud first! The next chapter shows you how to be successful no matter what and helps you move from mastery to artistry.

CHAPTER 9

THE FORTUNE IS IN PREMA

Your X factor lives to serve your audience. But as the adulation, ovations and encores pour in, even the humblest person can lose sight of this. *Prema* is our antidote. Prema is a Sanskrit word meaning love, not selfish love but a higher love. In this instance a love for your audience based on humility and respect.

If this sounds, umm, namby-pamby, take heed. PREMA Powerteam is an Italian motorsport team, competing as PREMAracing in the FIA Formula 2, FIA Formula 3 Championship and European Le Mans series. Not sure why the founders, Angelo Rosin and Giorgio Piccolo, chose the name PREMA but I can imagine they were aiming for something higher. Love of the sport, the competition, the fans.

With prema as your guide, in this chapter you'll learn how to humbly show up to your presentations, well prepared and practised in your X factor. Rachel Bourke, a Master Sales Trainer renowned for her practical, inspirational and no-nonsense style, says, '*The fortune is in the follow-up*'. I'll paraphrase that as; your fortune is in prema and practising these principles.

SHOWING UP WITH SERVICE IN MIND

X factor is there to help you serve your audience and your message. But showing up with service in mind, day in and day out, can be hard. Arthur C. Evans, chief executive officer of the American Psychological Association described living through the pandemic years as 'collective trauma'. Even First Lady Michelle Obama admits to suffering from low-grade depression. In an episode of *The Michelle Obama Podcast*, she elaborated: 'I'm waking up in the middle of the night because I'm worrying about something or there's a heaviness.' Feeling this 'heaviness', how can you as a professional show up with service with your X factor?

Look after yourself

Start with self-care, whatever that looks like for you. You cannot be useful to anyone as a husk of yourself. For me, it's trying to ground myself daily in meditation, journaling and exercise. It's also spending time with my family, connecting with friends and immersing myself in nature. But I'm the first to admit that most days I can do all of this, other days not so much. I'm learning to be more forgiving of myself, again an act of self-care. Michelle Obama shared, 'I try to make sure I get a workout in, although there have been periods throughout this quarantine where I just have felt too low.' So relatable.

Maslow's hierarchy of needs uses a pyramid to define the different levels of people's needs. This hierarchy includes physiological needs, safety needs, love and belonging needs, esteem needs and self-actualisation needs. Traditionally, Maslow's hierarchy places self-actualisation needs (fulfilment of one's talents and potentialities) at the top. But recent thinking has placed *service* at the very top of the hierarchy.

I now grapple with a more nuanced understanding of what service means. It is hard to let go of its action-focused trajectory. Even simple acts shift significantly when you see them both as acts of self-care and service. Serving others (no matter how small or humble the act) allows you to show up and gives you purpose and a sense of hope. A client describes it like this: 'Some days I get out of bed because my team is depending on me.'

I see you

Showing up with service in mind is also honouring and respecting your audiences.

Melbourne, where I live, has the unenviable record of having been the most locked down city in the world during the first two years of the pandemic (2020–21). It was tough and challenging for everyone, from parents struggling with home schooling and our senior citizens facing indefinite periods of loneliness and isolation, to people worried about how to make ends meet without an income.

One Sunday during lockdown, I opened my local newspaper and was touched by a public thank you. *Yes!* Of course it wasn't addressed to me alone. The state government was thanking us for how we'd faced those past few weeks with courage, with humility and with hope. But as one member of this audience, I felt honoured, recognised and respected. A government expressing its gratitude to its citizens for working hard to do the right thing. I felt teary reading it.

Now every time I'm physically in a room, I say, 'I want to take a moment to honour this moment, our being in a room together. It's a privilege I'll never take for granted again'. And I mean it with every fibre of my being. In my online sessions, I say, 'I want to honour our being together, the privilege of our being safe and able to attend. Thank you for your time and attention. I respect, appreciate and am grateful for it'.

Before 2020 I never made this explicit. I thought my actions demonstrated this. Sharing this gratitude in words with my audience is now also important. It frames the session for the audience, holds me as the presenter accountable and reminds me I am here to serve.

Bent knee

Every year *Forbes* publishes its tally of the world's billionaires. In 2022 they noted that the US$65 billion fortune of Changpeng Zhao, the Chinese-Canadian CEO of the cryptocurrency exchange Binance, makes him a crypto billionaire and the richest person in the digital currencies world. In response, Zhao tweeted, 'I only count what's in my wallet, which is not much at all'. I'm adding these hashtags to his statements: #stayhumble #staygrounded #keepitreal.

Owning your X factor requires both courage and humility — the courage to be fierce and fabulous and the humility to remain grounded. Hollywood megastar Halle Berry buys groceries with her kid, uses public transport and considers this behaviour normal. I love Dave Pell's newsletter *Next Draft*, in which he describes himself as 'the Internet's Managing Editor'. It's an audacious X factor, and what grounds this ironic claim is his writing, which is witty, insightful and absolutely brilliant!

Sometimes people mistake humility for having a low view of their own importance. But at its best humility is freedom from pride or arrogance. Perhaps Jeff Boss, author, leadership coach and former Navy SEAL, said it best in an article in *Forbes Online*: 'To be humble is not to think less of oneself, but to think of oneself less.' He adds, 'Humility is frequently associated with being too passive, submissive or insecure, but this couldn't be further from the truth. Instead, humble people are quite the opposite, confident and competent in themselves'. And likeable.

Another pillar of humility is to always be learning. **Your X factor is always a work in progress.** It's never complete. And you must always be open to feedback. In fact, you invite it and actively seek it. Think of feedback as a gift. After each presentation, select one or two people and ask them this specific question: 'What is one thing I can do better?' This simple question guarantees you will keep growing and succeeding.

When Walt Disney visited his theme park, he would always go down on his knees at every attraction so he could see what the children experienced. This is a useful metaphor for thinking about your X factor. Can you grow it on the intellectual version of a bent knee, so it always serves your audience?

ARTISTRY

The humble mobile that hangs over a baby's cot was one of the most radical art inventions ever. For thousands of years, sculptures were carved from heavy, inert material such as stone, marble or bronze. Alexander Calder wanted more. Art, he decided, was 'too static to reflect our world of movement'. In the 1930s Calder became one of the first artists to create works of art with moving parts. It was revolutionary.

Reimagining

Soon Calder was making wire sculptures suspended from the ceiling. Calder's work transformed twentieth-century notions of sculpture. His creations had people craning their necks to watch works of art that moved and changed before their eyes. Alexander Calder set art in motion. Every time you see a mobile hanging over a baby's cot you have Calder to thank.

The artist's eye reimagines the present, envisions the future and never stops challenging what is possible. Bring this mindset to your work as an X factor explorer.

This is how you can grow from amateur to master to artist. This trajectory depends on your interest, focus and ability to put in the hard yards. For those with an innate talent that can power them forward, the journey is swifter. But 'hard work beats talent when talent fails to work hard'. This idea was made popular by professional athletes, though it was first coined by high-school basketball coach Tim Notke. It applies equally to all fields of work and play.

Maybe you play violin in your city's symphony orchestra. Even if you're too modest to admit it, that would require a significant level of mastery. When you master your X factor you move into the realm of unconscious competence. You may not be able to unpick what you do and why. It becomes second nature. Anyone who has tried to glean a recipe from an intuitive cook will be familiar with this phenomenon. They don't follow recipes, use only rough measurements, and are guided by smell and look. Next, what sets artistry apart?

Curiosity

In the 1990s NASA commissioned George Land and Beth Jarman to design a test to measure the creative potential of their rocket scientists and engineers. The test measures divergent thinking, how to look at a particular problem and propose multiple solutions. In the test 98% of pre-schoolers measure at genius level. This then drops off alarmingly to just 2% for adults. The key difference is that kids, like artists, arrive at a solution, *but they don't stop there*. They keep looking at other ways to solve the same problem, whereas adults stop after the very first solution. Dr Land's advice for adults is to be less critical and more curious. Artistry requires curiosity.

Dame Zaha Hadid is one of the most famous architects in history. She was the first woman architect to win the prestigious Pritzker Architecture Prize. Hadid challenged the norms by taking strong materials like concrete and steel and using them to design buildings that appear both soft and flowing but also sturdy. Her style is futuristic, with curving facades and sharp angles, pushing spatial boundaries and inspiring awe. You would never pass one of her buildings without doing a double take, even if you are gormless about architecture. She was dubbed 'the queen of the curve' and her legacy continues to shape design and what is architecturally possible.

Artists like Hadid are curious and challenge the status quo and conventional thinking. In the Port House in Antwerp, Belgium, Hadid placed a modern 100-metre-long diamond-like glass-covered form that resembles the hull of a ship atop a historic former fire brigade building. This execution created one of the world's most interesting historical preservation projects. It's scarcely believable. Who would even think of the idea, then have the courage to realise it? This is creative genius in action.

The contrarian nature of artistry requires you to back yourself, even if no one else will.

Go bold and buck convention

Artistry requires you to go bold even when everyone else is screaming for you to go safe. Prepare to buck convention and resist well-intentioned opposition.

Red hair, red beard, dances theatrically. Who is this? A new Australian sports hero! On 14 June 2022 the Australian Socceroos were playing Peru in a World Cup qualifier decider. After 120 painful minutes, the qualification came down to a penalty shootout. Just one minute before the end of extra time Socceroos' coach Graham Arnold made a bold decision that had everyone falling off their seats.

Arnold brought in substitute goalkeeper Andrew Redmayne for the shootout. Genius or madness? With the weight of the nation's hopes on his shoulders, Redmayne made the magnificent match-winning save, sparking wild scenes of jubilation both on and off the field. Arnold's gamble paid off and the Socceroos qualified for a fifth straight World Cup.

Andrew Redmayne is now an Australian legend, icon and national hero. What it took was a moment of extraordinary boldness and courage from head coach Arnold.

Counterintuitive as it was and no one could guarantee it would pay off.

MY WISH FOR YOU

In 2014 I was invited to speak at the Ford Global Leadership Summit in Dearborn, Detroit. After months of preparation, I arrive in Dearborn a day before my speaking slot. The organisers take me aside and say, 'The leaders want to know why we brought a consultant all the way from Australia. Is she an automotive industry expert?' Er no, my car is silver, and it takes unleaded ... I think.

My heart skips a beat and my hands start shaking. I know that in a previous year the storytelling consultant was stopped and sent off from the stage after the first 30 minutes.

I know I must eat my own dog food and follow the advice I'd give any client: 'Open with your X factor.' Don't save the hanging upside down from a trapeze or getting shot out of a glitter cannon till the end. You won't make it that far. For me, as you know one of my X factors is storytelling. But I have nothing for this audience, only sweaty palms and a pounding heart.

That evening they take us in a bus with grills over the windows, bulletproof glass and armed security to gritty downtown Detroit. We go to the original Ford Piquette Avenue Plant museum, which showcases gleaming models of every car Ford has ever manufactured.

Something in the museum and the adrenaline rushing through my body triggers a primal memory from my past. I text my brother in India, and he responds with a photo and a (h)interesting fact that will save my life.

The next morning I enter the conference room, and this is what I open with:

> 'I want you to travel back in time with me to 1950s Madras, India. My grandfather is standing at the docks along with about ninety family members. A ship has just docked from Essex, England, carrying a precious cargo.
>
> 'Suddenly the crowd burst into loud cheers and applause as down the ramp rolls a gleaming 1949 Ford Prefect. My grandfather — his hobby was cars — had ordered a new car. My grandfather and seven of his closest male relatives

squeeze into the car, and the rest of the family follow on foot. A special wedding band playing ramshackle music has been employed to lead the car parade. People in Madras pour out onto the street or hang off their balconies and rooftops to watch the parade. Street urchins run besides the car all the way home, where the rest of the family is waiting to greet them all with flower garlands and clouds of fresh rose petals.

'The Ford Prefect became part of our family life. Every new baby, including me, was brought home from hospital in the car, which made a guest appearance at every wedding and the cycle of life at every funeral.

'Recently our Ford Prefect featured in the local newspaper. We are one of the only two families in present day Chennai, India, where the car has remained in the same family for four generations.

'So whatever it may look like on the outside, on the inside I am a fourth-generation Ford girl after all!'

I had goosebumps when I finished and could literally feel the room turning from ice cold into this warm golden-honey embrace that said, *you are one of us.* It turned out that many of the leaders in the room were also fourth-generation Ford people.

Secretly, on the inside, I also thought, *I'm so glad my grandfather didn't buy a Holden*!

The organisers invited me back four years in a row to present at their Global Leadership Summit.

That day X factor saved my life as a professional speaker. As my reader, I only have one wish for you: that with every presentation your 10% X factor delivers you a 100% result.

This is where your new journey begins, and we prepare to part ways. You probably have learned quite a lot about me through this book, but I also now know something about you. Don't panic, I'm not using Jedi mind tricks, but I can infer a couple of things about you just because you've come this far (that is, if you haven't jumped straight here from the start). You are a reader, you are probably already a high achiever (yes, blatant flattery) and you are hungry to make this work.

How can you leverage your knowledge to unleash this superpower? Like all superheroes, action is what drives you.

Where do you begin? My advice is simple. Once you have done the work in identifying your X factor statement, write down a commitment here and now on how you're going to use it.

I, _____, will use my X factor

_____
at this presentation event [name of event]

_____
on _____ [date].

Don't overthink it. Focus on the smallest micro action you can take to get started on your X factor. As James Clear, author of the bestseller *Atomic Habits*, reminds us, 'Successful people start before they are ready'.

Finally, these parting words of wisdom from Amanda Gorman, who at 22 became America's first-ever National Youth Poet Laureate. This line is from her poem 'The Hill We Climb'. 'There is always light. If only we're brave enough to see it. If only we're brave enough to be it.'

Now go out there and be the light with your X factor.

LET'S CONNECT

Every writer has but one wish: to be read. It is readers like you who make that wish come true. So, a giant thank you. I also have a small favour to ask of you. Please write a review of my book online. Reviews on Amazon seem to work best. Just saying. Authors like me depend on your word of mouth. But Good Reads is another terrific option. Your review could make a world of difference for me.

Of course, if you want to go rogue analogue, then raving about this book to everyone you meet for the next week would be welcome too. Or you could do both! Thank you.

I'd love to partner with you on this journey, so please connect with me on my website **yamininaidu.com.au** or on LinkedIn: **linkedin.com/in/yamininaidu**

I wish you all courage and good fortune in unleashing your X factor. I promise your life both professional and personal will never be the same.

With best wishes,
Yamini

ADDITIONAL RESOURCES

Paper copies on the following pages.

To download a copy, go to
xfactor.yamininaidu.com.au
or scan this QR code.

3X Super Steps Template

The 3X Super Steps process:

1. Gather
2. Zing
3. Craft

3X Super Step 1: Gather — **history/heritage**

Be specific and detailed. We want richness, juicy details and depth.

3X Super Step 1: Gather — **hobbies**

3X Super Step 1: Gather — (h)interesting facts

3X Super Step 2: Zing

1. **Highlight zing words (on your own, no template)**
2. **Create single circles and interlink circles (use template on next page)**
3. **Build shortlist word combinations (on your own, no template)**

3X Super Step 2: Zing — **create single circles** and interlink circles

1. Place each zing word in its own circle
2. One word or phrase per circle
3. Put as many words or phrases into circles as possible
4. Go for quantity
5. Review your zing words. Can any others be highlighted and added in circles?

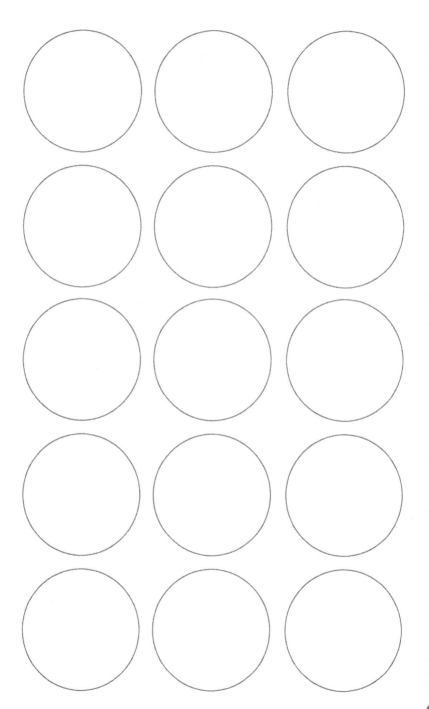

3X Super Step 2: Zing — create single circles and **interlink circles**

1. Combine three random single circles into interlinking circles
2. Go wild - as many combinations of words as possible
3. Work fast
4. Experiment go for quantity
5. Don't edit, this is your long list

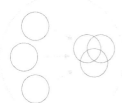

3X Super Step 3: **Craft**

100+ Banned X factor words

A
1. Activator
2. Adaptor
3. Adventurer
4. Advocate
5. Agile
6. Agitator
7. Alchemist
8. All formal job titles, period
9. Analyst
10. Author

B
11. Big picture thinker
12. Blogger
13. Board member
14. Business owner

C
15. Catalyst
16. Certified
17. Challenger
18. Champion
19. Change . . . maker, specialist, expert, agent etc.
20. Co-founder
21. Coach
22. Connector
23. Consultant
24. Content creator, producer
25. Conversationalist
26. Creative / Creator
27. Critical thinker
28. Curator

D
29. Designer
30. Developer
31. Director
32. Disruptor
33. Dreamer

E
34. Educator
35. Empowerer
36. Entrepreneur
37. Experienced
38. Expert

F
39. Facilitator
40. Founder
41. Futurist

G
42. Game Changer
43. General
44. Generator
45. Guide
46. Guru

H
47. Hacker

I
48. Ideas guy/person
49. Ideator
50. Innovator
51. Interpreter

L
52. Leader

M
53. Major
54. Maker (anything maker)
55. Master trainer
56. Maven
57. MC
58. Media commentator
59. Mediator
60. Mentor
61. Motivator
62. Mover and shaker

100+ Banned X factor words

O
64. Optimiser
65. Organiser
66. Out-of-the-box thinker

P
67. Passionate
68. Philosopher
69. Podcaster
70. Practitioner
71. President
72. Problem solver
73. Producer
74. Professional

R
75. Radical
76. Regenerator
77. Reinventor
78. Renaissance man
79. Researcher

S
80. Sense maker
81. Sherpa
82. Skilled
83. Social media anything (influencer, maven, creator etc)
84. Speaker
85. Specialist
86. Strategic
87. Strategist
88. Subject matter expert
89. Supervisor

T
90. Teacher
91. TED or TEDx speaker
92. Thinker
93. Thought leader
94. TikToker
95. Tracker
96. Trainer
97. Translator
98. Trusted adviser/partner

W
99. Writer

Y
100. YouTuber

- All martial arts–related terms, such as Karate master, black belt, Ninja etc.
- All animal names (unicorn of this, tiger of that etc.)
- All sports-related terms
- Hacking this list and adding 'er' etc at the end of words
- Portmanteaus (words blending two other words) like momager, purposologist, reviewed on a case by case basis. Portmanteaus like Brunch highly recommended in life.
- Transponster and other made-up words!

OTHER TITLES BY YAMINI NAIDU

yamininaidu.com.au

CPSIA information can be obtained
at www.ICGtesting.com
Printed in the USA
BVHW080718080323
659892BV00016B/119